Strategies for Effective Customer Education

Strategies for Effective Customer Education

Peter Honebein

American Marketing Association
Chicago, Illinois

NTC Business Books
a division of *NTC Publishing Group* • Lincolnwood, Illinois USA

Printed on recyclable paper

Library of Congress Cataloging-in-Publication Data

Honebein, Peter C., 1963–
    Strategies for effective customer education / Peter Honebein
       p. cm.
    "American Marketing Association."
    Includes index.
    ISBN 0-8442-3582-2 (alk. paper)
    1. Consumer education.   2. Customer relations.   I. Title.
TX335.H53 1996
641'.73—dc20   96-20664
                                              CIP

Published in conjunction with the American
Marketing Association, 250 South Wacker Drive,
Chicago, Illinois, 60606.

Published by NTC Business Books, a division of NTC Publishing Group,
4255 West Touhy Avenue,
Lincolnwood (Chicago, Illinois, 60646-1975, U.S.A.

6 7 8 9 BC 9 8 7 6 5 4 3 2 1

Contents

Chapter 2

DEFINING CUSTOMER EDUCATION 7

Chapter 3

ANALYZING PERFORMANCE PROBLEMS WITH CUSTOMERS AND PRODUCTS 23

Chapter 4

DRIVING FORCES FOR CUSTOMER EDUCATION 45

Chapter 5

THE PROCESS OF CUSTOMER EDUCATION 67

Chapter 6

PRODUCT SYSTEMS 91

Chapter 7

CUSTOMER EDUCATION SOLUTIONS 115

Chapter 8

IMPLEMENTING CUSTOMER EDUCATION PROGRAMS 137

Chapter 9

EVALUATING CUSTOMER EDUCATION PROGRAMS 165

Preface

My indoctrination into the powers of customer education began at a small camera store where I worked during high school and college. There I worked with one of the best teaching salespersons I know, Steven Underwood. Steven consistently sold more than any of the other salespeople at the store. His secret? He would spend most of his time teaching customers the art of good photography, including camera operations, lighting, film choice, and subject-matter composition. His customers were loyal, asked for him by name, and bought from him time and time again. (As a matter of fact, customers could not have had a better teacher—Steven is now a successful commercial photographer in San Francisco.)

What Steven found worked well for him was the process of customer education. In its simplest form, customer education aims to build customers' knowledge and skills with the products and services they buy. Customers who can use a product or service successfully are more likely to be satisfied customers, so customer education is an effective marketing strategy.

Why does customer education increase customer satisfaction? Because it is a marketing-based process that is about more than just selling products and services. It is about selling a system of solutions to help a customer resolve a need. A camera, for instance, can take a customer only so far in resolving the need to take quality photographs. Providing education about photography as part of the whole package ensures a complete system.

What I learned from Steven was customer education on the front line—supporting customers in their use of the product. After I graduated from college, I learned about the process of customer education from a different perspective: the fields of advertising and corporate communications. In these fields, customer education is a means of promoting and selling products. As I quickly learned, you must often teach the customer something before you get the sale commitment to buy the product.

Training magazine showed that sales in organizations providing customer education jumped nearly 20 percent between 1990 and 1994.[1] The report attributed this rise to the technological revolution. Complex, technical products require more hand-holding than the simpler products of the past. Selling solutions, not just products, also contributes to the rise, as does the need for companies to get close to customers, building long-term relationships rather than flash-in-the-pan associations. Customer education offers a solution to these needs. The opportunity for you to harness the power of customer education programs is now.

About This Book

Strategies for Effective Customer Education does not meddle with the details of writing instruction manuals; rather, it clearly and concisely maps out the big picture, linking the theory and practice that will lead your company's customer education efforts. It will help you conceptualize and plan strategies and foundations for building successful customer education programs in your company by bridging the gaps that exist between the disciplines of marketing, education, and customer service. After reading this book, you will be able to plan strategies that:

- Provide customers the knowledge they need to choose your product over the competition. This increases your sales and your bottom line.
- Ensure that customers can succeed with your products. This builds customer satisfaction and establishes customer relationships while reducing the costs to service customers.

- Raise barriers to competition by increasing switching costs, namely the retraining costs needed for learning a competitor's products.
- Enable you to develop and deliver quality solutions in your organization. This gives you the tools so you can effectively defend the plans you recommend to management, feel confident about your work, and be proud of the results you accomplish.

The intended audience for this book is anyone within an organization who manages or plans any form of communications with customers, especially the following:

- **Marketers,** including product managers, advertisers, public relations specialists, and salespeople
- **Trainers,** including instructional designers and technical writers
- **Customer service professionals,** including call center managers and service managers

The organization of this book loosely follows the systematic design of instruction, a generally accepted process of creating quality educational solutions (described in Chapter 3). The core components of the process are analysis, design, development, implementation, and evaluation. This process itself forms the basic foundation for customer education strategy, yet there are various nuances within each step of the process that contribute to the rigor your strategy will need.

Because this book follows a process, it is best read straight through the first time. Later, as you begin creating or revising programs, you will use it as a reference tool. The first two chapters will get you up to speed on the language, terms, and theory that drive the content of this book. The remaining chapters discuss the tools and models needed in each step of the instructional design process.

Chapter 1 forecasts what will happen with customer education in the face of projected changes in business, technology, and the marketplace.

Chapter 2 defines customer education. It first examines the core components of customer education—the customer, the domains of learning, and the process of education—and then covers the various forms of customer education, showing how they contribute to promoting a product or service, help structure buying decisions, and teach customers how to use products.

Chapter 3 explains the five steps of the instructional design process: needs analysis, design, development, implementation, and evaluation. Then it describes various tools you can use for identifying problems that might benefit from customer education. The key tool is gap analysis, which is the process of comparing the difference between what your customer is doing now and what your customer should be doing.

Chapter 4 explains the rationale for adopting customer education, linking needs to marketing, legal, and organizational forces. Through an analysis of the forces, you will be able to prioritize where you direct your customer education resources.

Chapter 5 links customer education to the sales process, embodied in the goal formation, acquisition, consumption, and disposition theory of consumer behavior. Through this chapter, you will learn to use tools that help you manage the scope of your customer education programs for each of your primary types of customers.

Chapter 6 outlines the product systems model and relates it to customer education strategy. Planning effective customer education is directly related to product design and customer support. If a product has poor ergonomics (or a bad user interface), then the need for customer education is heightened. If the product lacks sufficient customer education, then customer support bears the burden of resolving customer problems. Understanding the interaction of these three elements—product design, education, and support—is imperative for effective customer education.

Chapter 7 presents five case studies of companies that have invested in customer education and have seen a return on that investment. Each case study describes the needs the company faced, its programs and solutions, and the results the solutions delivered.

Chapter 8 discusses a process for implementing customer education programs, following a standard marketing model: positioning, pricing, and promoting. It also covers delivery of customer education and how to avoid the common pitfalls.

Chapter 9 describes an evaluation process that examines how well customers like programs, how much they learn from programs, how they apply what they learn, and what return on investment their learning ultimately provides.

Acknowledgments

April 6, 1992: That is when my quest to write a book on customer education began. I know this because my trusty Macintosh keeps for me the creation dates of every document I write. The first outline I wrote to flush out my initial ideas on customer education was created on this date. Now, four years later, my quest is complete.

Over the past four years, many people have been sources of inspiration, guidance, and ideas for the content of this book. This project began while I was a graduate student in the instructional systems technology Ph.D. program at Indiana University. Tom Duffy and Ivor Davies, professors of instructional design, provided encouragement and guidance in sorting through the linkages between instructional design and customer education.

Richard Olshavsky, professor in the School of Business at Indiana University, was the first to show me the relationship between customer education and choice behavior. His mentoring in the comprehensive theory of choice stretched my ideas in many new directions, helping me figure out how to integrate customer education into the world of marketing.

The opportunity to make this book a reality began when the American Marketing Association ran one of my first articles on customer education in *Marketing News.* "If You Teach Them, Will They Come?" *The Service Edge* newsletter, published by Lakewood Publications, followed up this article and interviewed me for a feature article on customer education. Rosanne Alonzi, from the Institute for International Research, read the article and was excited enough by the concept that she organized the first-ever conference on customer education with me as the chairperson. The presenters at this conference contributed significantly to my development of numerous customer education ideas as well as several of the case studies in this book: Dorthy Hellberg of Fisher-Rosemount, William Hitchcock of EDS, Carl Binder of Product Knowledge Systems, John Landon of Pfizer Animal Health, Gary Butler of NYNEX, Cyndy Fitzgerald and Celeste Boyer of Microsoft, Phil Heinz of 3M, Gerald Mielke of H.B. Fuller, and Linda Schleifer of Safety-Kleen.

Carl Cox of Boeing, Shirley Rogers and Lorraine Wilkin of Fitch, Morris Walberg of Hewlett-Packard and Tom Taggart of Charles Schwab made time for interviews and helped me track down good examples of their own customer education programs. Several clients and business partners have provided me the opportunity to learn about instructional design and customer education firsthand, whether as the designer of an educational program or a member of a product development team. In the interest of confidentiality, they shall remain anonymous. The Indiana University library and the University of Nevada, Reno library were primary sources for most of the published material that helped shape my ideas. I thank all those people who have taken the time to publish their experiences with customer education.

Numerous people have read various portions of this book over the past four years, guiding my ideas and encouraging my progress: Roy Cammarano, Libby Dodd, Karen Felker, Barry Fishman, Andy Hill, Carl Honebein, Jonathan Price, Richard Rutherford, Tom Welsh, and Gil Zeimer.

Thanks also to Rich Hagle of NTC Business Books and Francesca van Gorp of the American Marketing Association. Their vision and guidance have made this book a reality.

It is one's family, however, that loses the most during the writing of a book. In the past year alone, my wife, Beth, has given birth to a child, developed her own business, and put up with a husband who travels on business too much and sequesters himself in his office on evenings, weekends, and holidays to pound out yet another couple thousand words. Her patience and support for the project are greatly appreciated.

The Future of Customer Education

The next five years promise increasing need for customer education. No, customers are not getting dumber; rather, they are getting smarter as a result of the information age. The problem, however, is that information alone is often goal-free. The sender of the information does not thoughtfully consider the purpose of the information and the results the information was supposed to provide. As such, customers are often left to their own devices to figure out the meaning of information. They must grapple with it for a long time to draw any benefit from it. Through this process, the conclusions they draw from the information might bear no relationship to the intentions of the sender. The result is communication that is neither effective nor efficient.

To overcome these problems, customer education must structure information to attain specific goals. The process of customer education, as described in this book, provides the level of structure necessary to achieve your desired communication results.

The customer education solutions you develop now and in the future will relate directly to trends in the marketplace. Your ability to recognize and ride these trends will contribute to customer education solutions that are effective, efficient, and appealing.

Trend 1: Knowledge-Based Business

Two noted futurists, Stan Davis and Jim Botkin, predict that our economy is shifting from being information-based to being knowledge-based.[1] Information is often a by-product of company operations. Yet if a company can harness that information and organize it in a meaningful way, it becomes knowledge. A knowledge-based economy, according to Davis and Botkin, is one filled with "smart" products and services that promote learning as well as embrace learning.

Examples of these products? How about a tennis racket whose strings glow to indicate where the player hit the ball. The feedback of where the ball hits the racket is critical in helping the player improve his or her tennis stroke. The racket, in effect, becomes not only the player's tool to play the game, but also the player's coach. Other examples include diapers that change color when wet, clothes that adjust themselves depending on the temperature, and tires that inform drivers of their air pressure.

Businesses that embrace learning can also use knowledge from customers to provide better levels of service. Ritz-Carlton hotels keep track of their customers' preferences, such as amenities they request, to ensure those amenities are made available to them automatically at every Ritz-Carlton property around the world. Credit card companies learn about the spending patterns of their customers to keep a watchful eye for breaks in that pattern that might indicate credit card fraud.

If businesses are to become knowledge-based, then they must undergo a change in mindset about their purpose. According to Davis and Botkin:

> Seeing customers as learners requires a major change in thinking. But over the next two decades businesses will come to think of their customers as learners and of themselves as educators. They will promote the learning experience for profit, and their customers will profit from that experience.[2]

For businesses to think of themselves as educators, they must consider the needs of their customers and the tasks customers wish to accomplish. Needs provide the reason for education, but tasks are the building blocks for what that education should look like and feel like. Most businesses are good at recognizing customer needs. However, to create a knowledge-based business, you must develop the means to examine the tasks of customers and look for ways to support those tasks. Chapters 5 and 6 provide models for you to begin thinking about how to capture and understand the tasks of your customers.

Trend 2: Solutions Selling and Relationship Marketing

Customers have learned that they no longer want just products. They want solutions to problems. Sales and marketing departments in companies around the world are continually realizing this as a basic customer need. As such, they have repositioned their products or are beginning to reposition them, as solutions. They are also modifying sales strategies to sell the solution, not just the box. The rise in the solutions-oriented selling strategies companies adopt, such as consultative selling, non-manipulative selling, and power-base selling, are all indicators that this shift is taking place.

An important element of any solution, of course, is the ability of customers to make the solution work. Therefore, companies who have positioned their products as solutions ensure that education is an integral part of what they sell. They discuss education with their customers, include it in their proposals, and ensure that it meets the customer's need for a solution.

A by-product of providing solutions to customers is the opportunity to form a strong relationship with customers. Marketing guru Regis McKenna has written several books and articles on building relationships with customers. One key point he makes is that the transfer of knowledge between buyer and seller—education—is a necessary element for building strong relationships with customers:

> To develop new markets, it is essential for companies to take the time to educate customers. When microprocessors were first introduced, in the early 1970s, few customers recognized the value of the new chips. People are resistant to change, and the idea of programmable chips was foreign. Even many engineers believed that the microprocessor was a marketing gimmick.
>
> So Intel, the first company to market microprocessors, had to do a massive education job. It ran advertisements filled with suggested

applications for the new product. It distributed booklets containing descriptions of actual applications, from electronic games to blood analyzers, from milking machines to satellites. Most important, Intel ran seminars for potential corporate customers. In the first few years, Intel ran hundreds of these seminars worldwide. At each seminar, Intel first presented a corporate overview, usually given by a top company executive. Next, an Intel marketing manager would give a presentation on the marketing value of microprocessor-based products. Finally, Intel engineers would describe the technical details of the microprocessors. Most of the early customers ordered only a few microprocessor chips. But as the education campaign continued, Intel attracted more and more high-volume users.[3]

If you look back on your life, consider the respect, appreciation, and trust you have for anyone who has helped you learn in a meaningful way. It might have been a professor at your university, a manager who became your mentor, or a friend who helped you cope with a difficult problem. These people have a special meaning in your life because they helped you learn and grow. Through customer education, businesses can have a similar impact on their customers, making the bonds that link buyer and seller stronger because of trust and sharing, rather than solely because of need.

Trend 3: Distribution of Knowledge through Technology

Technologies such as the Internet and the fax machine are enabling businesses to distribute knowledge to customers faster than ever before. The days of waiting for a product brochure are now over, because you can now log into a company's World Wide Web home page and get the knowledge you need at the touch of a key. Fax-back systems where you have documents sent to your fax machine automatically by dialing a central number and specifying the documents you want, is another means of rapid distribution. Customers will always have the need for just-in-time knowledge to solve problems they are working on today. These systems facilitate rapid access.

In addition to supplying pre-sales product brochures and data sheets through these systems, companies are using the Internet to give customers access to technical manuals and other instructional materials. As networked information systems become more advanced, the current text-and-graphics nature of the Internet will expand to include videos, sound, and animation. Your customer's desktop computer will enable him or her to access training videos from a central database or subscribe to live broadcasts of training classes over a distance education network. The high travel costs associated with delivering and attending customer education programs are pushing both companies and customers to design distance education solutions for their programs.

However, as the channel for providing educational programs remotely opens up, the need for tools to help customers find and select the appropriate solution will increase. Search systems, smart program guides, and automated curriculum planners will help customers determine their learning needs and help the customer chose the educational programs that will resolve those needs.

Increasing the speed with which customers can access knowledge will also increase the speed required to create it. Paper-based resources are often updated only on a yearly basis, if that frequently. Customers expect these materials to be somewhat out of date because it is inefficient and expensive for the media to respond any faster. Now expectations are changing. If you deliver information electronically, customers expect it, even demand it, to be up-to-date. After all, it is electronic. It does not need to be printed, packaged, and mailed.

To keep up with customers' expectations for speed, you need to reengineer the infrastructure within your company to handle knowledge more efficiently. As a rule of thumb, new knowledge should be created only once and owned by one person, then repackaged into other forms. Repackaging should rely on automation, because each time human hands touch the knowledge delays its delivery to customers. To facilitate this, the knowledge companies create should be graded to reflect its volatility. Packagers of knowledge should know what knowledge is likely to be static and what knowledge is likely to be ever changing to ensure the systems and methods they develop can respond effectively.

Trend 4: Outsourcing of Employee Training

Who will train the nation's workers if companies continue to downsize their training departments out of existence? Most likely, it will be the businesses that sell companies their systems and tools. If a company hires EDS to design and develop a next-generation order-processing system, EDS will train the workers to use this new system. If a company buys a Hewlett-Packard computer system, HP will teach the system administrators UNIX. If a casino buys International Game Technology's (IGT) slot machines and systems, IGT will teach the casino's floor people how to manage and maintain the machines.

Business customers can reduce the workload of their training departments if the vendors who supply the tools and systems take the responsibility for teaching employees. It is also more efficient and effective to rely on the vendor for these services, because the vendor is the expert. Adding another layer of complexity in repackaging the knowledge—your training department—only compounds the issue.

Vendors must ensure the quality of the training programs they offer customers. Many world-class companies have worked long and hard to understand the difference between good training and bad training, so do not think that you can get away with hacking together a solution. You need to make sure the programs you offer companies and employees are well designed and well developed to meet certain standards of quality. Without the quality, your programs will not be accepted. Additionally, many companies have established specific formats and methods of delivering training. To ensure consistency with their existing programs, you should be prepared to customize your courses for the customer.

If you are a vendor who is downsizing your own training department, stop! Consider redeploying these people into a more strategic role by focusing them on customer education. They know your business and they know how to develop training that will lead your customer education efforts into the future.

Defining Customer Education

Customer education is not an event. It is a process. It exists throughout a customer's relationship with your company: before, during, and after the sale. It systematically links the activities of marketing, training, and customer support in order to meet customers' ongoing needs for understanding, application, and success—whether they are operating a new product, understanding a new technique, or learning how to run a business better. At its best, the process of customer education operates to continuously narrow the gap between your customers' knowledge about your product and a sale.

Any discussion of customer education can begin with a ubiquitous example: product instructions. The purpose of product instructions is to teach a customer how to use a product. For instance, you will find tea-making instructions on every Lipton tea bag label, multivolume user manuals in computer software boxes, and assembly instructions with the latest toys for your kids.

Product instructions are the place to start, but they are definitely not the place to stop. Videotapes, classes, advertisements, workshops, seminars, press releases, user bulletins, hands-on training, telephone support, computer training, multimedia, World Wide Web home pages, and company universities all enter the mix of vehicles on which education travels. Companies expect these efforts to profoundly impact customer satisfaction and ultimately lead to repeat business. Thus customer education might best be summarized as follows:

> Customer education is the process by which companies systematically share their knowledge and skills with external customers to foster the development of positive customer attitudes.

In other words, to have happy satisfied customers who buy and use your products (positive customer attitudes), a company must provide an array of need-driven educational experiences throughout the company's relationship with the customer. Some of these experiences might be promotional, providing customers the knowledge and skill they need to make a buying decision. Other experiences will be related to the product, providing customers sufficient knowledge and skills to use the product successfully. Customer education wraps together all the relevant philosophies, strategies, and tactics from the fields of marketing, education, and customer service to help companies plan, develop, and implement appropriate educational experiences.

Who Is the Customer?

The term *customer* has many meanings. Peter Drucker, in his book *Managing for Results,* speaks of the two types of customers every business has; the buyer and the distribution channel. For customer education, this translates into three kinds of customers: reseller, buyer, and user.

A **reseller** buys a product from you, then sells it to another person (another reseller or perhaps the end user). Examples of resellers include distributors, retailers, and catalogers.

A **buyer** is a customer who assumes the buying responsibility for another person but does not consume the product. Some call this the dog food model. People buy dog food but they are not the ultimate consumer. The dog is. Other examples of buyers include purchasing agents, managers, and people who give gifts.

A **user** is a customer who uses the product. Users are the ones who prepare it, eat it, assemble it, fix it, maintain it, and trash it. Users are sometimes also the ones who buy the product.

As shown in Exhibit 2–1, knowing how your product moves from your loading dock into the hands of the user defines whom you need to educate.

Exhibit 2–1   Paths of Distribution through the Three Types of Customers

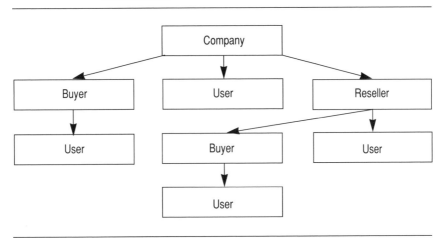

And knowing this leads you to identifying the knowledge gap between your product and those people and, thus, the learning needs of those people. Put these two together, and you have the foundation for a strategy.

Apple Computer has customer education systems in place to address the needs of customers at all three levels. Apple's primary means of distribution is through resellers, who in turn distribute products to buyers and users. So they have reseller education programs that teach resellers facts about products, how to use products, and how to sell the products to buyers and users. Apple's key account sales force keeps buyers in companies, such as management information systems (MIS) managers, informed of new products and strategies for new systems for the users in their organizations. For direct-to-user sales, Apple provides user manuals and interactive demonstrations with the products and sponsors the Apple Training Alliance, a group of third-party individuals and organizations certified to teach customers how to use Apple products.

The Link to Marketing

Customer education is first and foremost a marketing tool. The keystones of the marketing mix are the four Ps: product, promotion, price, and physical distribution. Wedged somewhere between product and promotion sits customer education. It is part of the product to the extent that it is a part of the benefit given to the customer to fill a particular need. It is part of promotion to the extent that it communicates information that enables or encourages the customer to make a decision to buy.

PRODUCT

Whether it is something tangible, such as a car or a container of ice cream, or intangible, such as legal advice, the product is at the heart of every marketing transaction. It is what you pay for.

Unless it is a pure commodity, a product or a "whole product" contains all the components that enable the customer to realize its benefits successfully. These components typically include the following:

- Physical product
- Spare parts
- Installation and/or field assembly
- Service
- Warranty
- Catalog data and sales brochures, advertising
- Instructions for use
- Instructions for user maintenance
- Instructions for factory-supplied service
- Shipping package
- Display package
- Labels, warning, and other on-product messages

Thus, customer education is as much a component of a product as its shipping package. Both are necessary to assure successful and proper use. Here are four examples showing how companies have made customer education integral parts of their products.

Smartguard. In recent years, pepper sprays have become popular as a means of self-defense. Pepper spray is an aerosol that, when sprayed in the face of an assailant, causes tearing and choking, rendering the assailant incapacitated for several minutes.

Typically, pepper spray comes only with instructions on the side of the can or on the back of the blister pack telling you how to point and shoot. But Smartguard sells more than just pepper spray; it sells a four-piece safety system including a safety training manual, a videotape, a training canister, and the actual pepper spray itself. The video features an experienced police officer showing you how to use the pepper spray, pointing out spray patterns and effective defensive techniques. The training canister, containing nonactive ingredients, allows you to practice using the device on your friends and family. Smartguard sends customers the message that only practice will prepare you for an emergency and supports that message with the appropriate customer education tools.

Grease Monkey. Grease Monkey is a 10-minute oil change franchise, but it is more than just a place to get your oil changed. Technicians meticulously perform about 30 separate checks to make sure basic auto parts are properly filled (e.g., ball joint grease, window washer fluid, and differential fluid) and in working order. Grease Monkey sells a service, not a product. Thus, their customer education activities focus on helping the customer understand that service rather than how to use a product.

Technicians at Grease Monkey begin the education process by showing customers their cars' air filter and breather units and advising them about whether they are dirty enough to warrant changing. The same process is done for the differential fluid and succeeding maintenance steps. Grease Monkey's other customer education solutions include a series of booklets explaining oil changes, types of oil, air filters, headlamps, differentials, and a host of other subjects related to general automobile maintenance. These materials are similar to the Shell Answerbooks that were popular many years ago.

Obviously, both the personal attention from the technician and the booklets are attempts to sell additional services. However, what you learn from the ten minutes you spend at Grease Monkey makes you feel good about what you are doing for your car.

Safety-Kleen. Safety-Kleen Corp. is in the business of recycling hazardous wastes. Its clients range from large manufacturing companies down to local gas stations. Much of Safety-Kleen's business (and the waste its customers' produce) is regulated by federal and state agencies, such as the Occupational Safety and Health Administration (OSHA) and the Environmental Protection Agency. As such, Safety-Kleen has had to navigate through complex regulations to avoid penalties. To ensure that the waste they receive from customers complies with government regulations as well as to build strong customer relationships, Safety-Kleen offers seminars to help its customers learn how to comply with the regulations. Over 60,000 companies have participated in the 1,000 annual seminars Safety-Kleen conducts nationally. The result is better-educated customers who have remained loyal clients to Safety-Kleen services.

Boeing. Because aircraft have always been on the leading edge of technology, Boeing has a long history of customer education. In 1917, Boeing started training customers in aircraft maintenance, flight operations, and ground operations. According to Carl Cox, a customer education specialist at Boeing, customer education is an integral part of the whole product. At the time the first plane is delivered to a customer, Boeing must have flight crews trained to fly the plane, ground crews trained to service the aircraft, and maintenance crews trained to maintain the plane. Without this training, the plane will not fly.

Customers are very clear about the training they expect from Boeing before they receive delivery of an aircraft. Using a five-level training model developed by the American Transportation Association, customers specify the training they want in the aircraft purchase contract. For maintenance training, the levels customers expect Boeing to provide include the following:

- General familiarization, for management and non-maintenance employees
- Ramp and transit, for maintenance workers who turn around an aircraft during a short interim stop
- Line and base, for workers who perform overnight and extended aircraft maintenance

The other levels, specialized course and overhaul, are typically conducted by the customer or other vendors.

PROMOTION

Promotion is obviously an opportunity for customer education. Complex products and unique innovations can require extended up-front time on the part of a salesperson to educate the customer before purchase. For the sake of efficiency, adopting specific educational techniques and instructional strategies can accelerate the buying decision. When it comes to promotion, customer educators have a unique mindset. Rather than selling, they see themselves as teaching the customer to buy.

Sony. Although best known for consumer products, Sony is involved in many businesses, including industrial video. Industrial video includes video camera, video recorder, and video editing products aimed at educational institutions, corporations, and independent video producers. In an exhibit at an educational technology trade show, Sony was introducing its new line of video editors. In its booth, Sony had several of the new editors set up on tables with chairs in front of them. Customers were invited to take a seat and "test drive" the editor. A Sony sales representative or product specialist sat with the customer to teach him or her how to make basic edits. Through this process, customers not only learned about the new technology, but also developed basic skills to use the technology and judge its ease of use.

Merrill Lynch. Merrill Lynch is a large, diversified financial services company. Its primary business is investor services, buying and selling stocks, bonds, mutual funds, and other investment instruments for customers. As a means to attract new customers, Merrill Lynch sponsors what it calls 'public education' to educate the general public about the world of finance and investments. Merrill Lynch's customer education strategy has two components. First, there are brochures with titles such as "Understanding Options," "How Over-the-Counter Securities Are Traded," and "What Is Margin?" Second, Merrill Lynch sponsors investment seminars delivered by account executives and other investment professionals. The seminars focus on both general investment topics and special topics such as tax law changes. The responsibility for this promotional customer education strategy is assumed by Merrill Lynch's advertising department.[1]

Customer education is a continuum from product to promotion, with the Smartguard defense system, Grease Monkey's services, Safety-Kleen's seminars, and Boeing's aircraft at the product end and Sony's trade show sessions and Merrill Lynch's investment seminars at the promotion end. Between these extremes are many examples of customer education that consist of a mixture of promotional and product aims.

What Can Customers Learn?

All aspects of marketing involve meeting customer needs. For customer education, these needs involve what the customer knows and feels about your product. When your customer learns something, such as the signal-to-noise ratio of a new CD player, how to assemble a child's new bicycle, or a preference for Dryer's strawberry ice cream, what kind of information is involved? One simple model is that the mind processes this information into three distinct domains of learning: knowledge, skills, and attitudes.

KNOWLEDGE

Knowledge is information stored in a person's mind through a process of remembering or understanding.[2] It has four aspects: facts, procedures, concepts, and principles.

- **Factual knowledge** is knowing a specific object, stating the nomenclature of an instrument, or recalling a past event or experience. A customer who states, "This CD player has a signal-to-noise ratio of 90 to 1," is recalling factual knowledge.
- **Procedural knowledge** is knowing the sequence or procedure to accomplish a given task. Knowing the steps to program a video cassette recorder with a remote control is an example of procedural knowledge.
- **Conceptual knowledge** is the ability to define phenomena or to recognize or give examples of phenomena. An example of conceptual knowledge is knowing what a remote control is.
- **Principle knowledge** is the rules and principles that predict or explain outcomes. An example of principle knowledge is a customer knowing that pressing the "on" button of the remote control will turn the television on.

SKILLS

Skills are a person's actions and reactions developed through practice and experience. They enable people to do something with their knowledge. The four aspects of skills are thinking, acting, reacting, and interacting.

- **Thinking, or cognitive, skills** are the abilities to make decisions and solve problems. Thinking might involve choosing an existing procedure and applying it to a problem or inventing a new procedure if one does not exist.
- **Acting, or behavioral or psychomotor,** skills are the abilities

to perform a physical action. Typing, running, or manipulating objects with one's hands are all example of acting skills.

- **Reactive skills** are the abilities to regulate one's self. Personal control, values, and attitudes are all reactive skills. An example of a reactive skill is a customer's choice to avoid using a product in a dangerous way, such as using a sharp knife as a screwdriver.
- **Interactive skills** are the abilities to deal with others. This includes good manners, pleasant verbal habits, leadership, and supervision.

ATTITUDES

Attitudes are a person's choices, values, or feelings.[3] Attitudes cause a person to act or think in a particular way. The three facets of attitudes are consistency, feelings, and readiness.

- **Consistency** is a person's desire for predictable beliefs and actions. A person who has learned to be loyal to a product, such as always buying Ford automobiles because he or she believes they are great cars, is exhibiting consistency.
- **Feelings** are a person's response to liking or disliking something. For instance one customer might love your product, but another customer might hate it.
- **Readiness** is a person's disposition toward a certain course of action. Choosing to learn how to use a new software package or making the decision to buy a product are two examples of a person's readiness.

What kinds of knowledge and skills do companies share with customers, and how do they affect customer attitudes? Personal selling provides a good example. What do salespeople do to get a sale? First, of course, they have to find a customer and determine the customer's needs. Next, they must send the customer literature about the product and possibly suggest to the customer some other reading material from the library. Then the customer comes to the store to see how the product works. The salespeople have to demonstrate the product for the customer and perhaps teach the customer how to work it. After the customer leaves the store to check out the competition, he or she calls the salesperson back to inquire about some specifications. The customer then returns to buy the product.

What are customers doing during these interactions with the salesperson? They are doing different kinds of learning. They learn facts about the product when they read the product brochure. They learn skills when the salesperson shows them how to work the product. And throughout the sales process, they form attitudes about the product itself through feelings of liking or disliking, then by making the decision to buy.

What is important in this story is that before customers learn an attitude, they learn knowledge and skills. Knowledge and skills are often prerequisites for attitude change. Thus, by sharing your knowledge and skills with customers, you can facilitate the development of positive customer attitudes.

Bridging the Gap between the Customer and Your Product

A gap exists between the customer and the knowledge, skills, and attitudes the customer desires or you desire the customer to possess. Consider the following gaps:

- A customer does not know about your product, and you need to make him or her aware of it.
- A customer wants to buy a product, and you need to convince him or her that yours is the one.
- A customer needs to learn to use your product, and you need to teach him or her.

How do you bridge these gaps in order to deliver knowledge, skills, and attitudes to customers? Through the process of education.

Education is a structured process of helping people acquire knowledge, skills, and attitudes. As shown in Exhibit 2–2, the process begins with a goal, such as to assemble a product. It continues with one or more learning events to achieve the goal, such as a training class or instruction manual. Finally, at the end of the process there is an assessment of whether the learner achieved the goal: a correctly assembled product.

Exhibit 2–2   The Educational Process

GOALS

The goals you specify for the educational process can have varying levels. They can be tactical or strategic. A **tactical goal** describes a specific task a customer will be able to accomplish once the educational process is complete. Here are some examples of tactical goals:

- Safely operate a gas-powered chain saw
- Ensure compliance with federal, state, and local hazardous waste laws
- Diagnose causes of instrument failures

A **strategic goal** describes a specific business result a company expects the educational process to deliver. Here are some examples of strategic goals:

- Increase repeat sales to existing customers
- Reduce customer calls to technical support specialists
- Deliver a turn-key solution to the customer

LEARNING EVENTS

Learning events are those methods by which you communicate knowledge, skills, and attitudes to your customers in order to achieve the goals. Training is the most typical learning event, although many people mistakenly equate training and education. In fact, education is a process, whereas training is an event. Here are some of the learning events common to customer education:

- Package instructions
- Instruction manuals
- Instructor-led courses and workshops
- Sales calls
- Trade show booths
- Advertisements
- World Wide Web home pages

ASSESSMENT

Assessment closes the educational process loop. It determines whether the learning events caused accomplishment of the specified goals. The typical measures for assessment include quality, quantity, cost, and time. Here are some examples of how the goals described above might be assessed:

- Five customers were injured by chain saws in 1996—this is 20 percent fewer than 1995 injuries.
- All customers (100%) are now in compliance with federal, state, and local laws.
- Technicians correctly diagnose failures more than 95 percent of the time.
- Average repeat orders in 1996 is five, up 35 percent from 1995.
- Technical support calls have been reduced by 10 percent.
- No installations required the presence of a service technician.

To get a better sense of the educational process as it relates to the customer, recall the sales example represented earlier. The process the salesperson employed to get the sale was an educational process. There was a goal (close the sale) and a set of educational events to achieve the goal: product literature, reading materials, demonstrations, one-on-one discussions. The assessment of the process was when the customer bought the product. Once the customer achieved the original goal, the goal is modified to, "Maintain a profitable relationship with the customer," and the educational process continues to meet the needs of the customer. Because it is a process, education never stops. What happens if the process does stop? Customers fail to use your products properly, you lose contact with them, or they may be lost to the competition.

Forms of Customer Education

The basic tenets of customer education manifest themselves in many different forms. Knowing these forms will help you better understand the breadth of customer education across different industries and professions. In these settings, you will find these forms of customer education stimulating sales, building trust, and increasing satisfaction under many different names.

STIMULATING SALES

Customer education as a means to stimulate sales has long been a staple for businesses. Virtually any form of marketing communication with a customer, whether through advertising, collateral, sales promotion, publicity, or personal selling, has an educational purpose. A national survey conducted by the advertising agency Needham, Harper & Steers, found that 70 percent of consumers surveyed agreed that information from advertising helps them make better buying decisions.[4] Advertising guru David Ogilvy stressed the need for customers to learn an attitude through advertising when he wrote, "When I write an advertisement, I don't want you to tell me you find it 'creative.' I want you to find it so interesting that you *buy the product.*"[5]

Salespeople have always been, in one form or another, the carriers of knowledge and skills to help customers learn. According to Regis McKenna, the role of the salesperson is that of educator. In describing the salesperson of now and in the future, McKenna writes that:

> The salesperson as "convincer" or "closer" of orders will go the way of the slide rule and instead become synonymous with "service." The salesperson will carry information, education, training, detailed design, quality, and reliability information. He or she will be the link between the product design, the factory, and the customer.[6]

Insurance agents have long practiced this philosophy. John Church, an insurance agent in Florida, firmly believes that his role is as teacher of insurance products and services. During his visits with customers, Church helps customers understand not only the products available for a specific need, but also the principles behind the products, such as risk ratings, premium cost, and procedures for filing claims. Church says that an educated client is a satisfied client, and that the time he spends with a client as a teacher is time well spent.[7]

BUILDING TRUST

Not all forms of customer education contain blatant sales messages. Customer education packaged in the form of consumer information or consumer education raises the perceived quality of the content by removing the marketing bias and slant from company-sponsored materials. Consumer researcher Paul Bloom calls consumer education:

> The process by which people learn the workings of the marketplace so they can improve their ability to act as purchasers or consumers of those products and services they deem most likely to enhance their well being.[8]

Consumer education serves a long-term, strategic purpose: To help customers become better customers, thus establishing a level of trust between the company and the consumer. Companies often possess knowledge that is beneficial to customers. After all, companies interact with thousands of customers everyday and conduct significant research to develop their products. Therefore, they typically are experts in a particular domain. No one would disagree that Eli Lilly is an expert in the treatment of diabetes through its experience with its Humulin product, or that Fleet Finance is an expert in consumer finance through its experience loaning people money.

This expert knowledge can make it easier for customers to do business with a company and stimulate awareness and resolution of generally accepted needs. If Fleet Finance teaches customers the basics of financial management, the likelihood of loan defaults and slow payments will fall, reducing collection costs for Fleet Finance. If the *New England Journal of Medicine* announces that strict control of diabetes reduces complications from the disease, then Eli Lilly is in the position to teach customers how to develop more compliant regimens, which will increase sales of its Humulin products. Companies see these opportunities as win-win situations. Customers acquire knowledge that will benefit them, and the companies realize a gain on their bottom line.

Consumers and consumer advocates, however, do not always perceive this as a win-win situation. They claim that greed is the companies' driving force for sharing knowledge and that this type of knowledge should be treated as suspect. To buffer these charges, companies partner with nonprofit organizations to give credibility to their message. The message consumers get is that if the National Consumers League thinks that Fleet Finance's consumer education programs are free from bias, then they must be okay. The American Diabetes Association offers the same level of credibility for certain materials Eli Lilly offers customers.

Related to consumer education is customer training. This form of customer education has been devised by human resources departments that are seeking to expand their role beyond their own employees. Through customer training, companies teach customers more general, non–product specific knowledge and skills. This includes such things as business processes and methods with which a company has experience. Often, customer training is when

> an employer invites some of its most important customers to participate in all aspects of training—including management development,

team building, and value setting—to promote more open communication, increase learning, and build commitment. The end result: a
bond between the company and its customers that can become the
foundation for long-term competitive advantage.[9]

General Electric (GE) incorporates customer training into programs
at its Management Development Institute in Crotonville, New York. GE
invites customers to its famous workout sessions to do such things as
challenge their existing relationship with GE and to work together on
better ways of improving systems linking the customer and GE. From
these exercises, customers gain insight on the way GE runs its business,
while GE learns about how customers think, their markets, and their
managerial processes. With this knowledge, (GE can set about aligning
its management systems with those of the customer, fostering the development of both personal and organizational relationships.[10]

A cross between customer training and consumer education is
known as client education, or, in the context of health care, patient
education. Client education is associated with professional business services. Lawyers, accountants, and other professionals offer clients
consultations, booklets, and seminars that help them understand the
workings of the profession. Patient education is associated with medical
services. Health care professionals and companies spend much of their
time educating patients about their health and treatment regimens. In
fact, federal legislation in 1990 mandated that pharmacists provide
counseling to their patients.

INCREASING SATISFACTION

Ensuring that customers are successful with a product once they have it
in hand is the key to increasing satisfaction. Through product training,
companies teach customers how to use a product or service. It is probably the best understood of all the forms of customer education, because
all customers need to learn how to use the products they buy. Whether
the product is a plane, train, automobile, computer, dishwasher, cord-
less telephone, box of pancake mix, or a little old tea bag, there will be
some type of instruction to teach customers how to use it. A unique
product training approach is Ferrari's Mugello Scholarship program.
Buyers of a new Ferrari 512TR are invited to Ferrari's Mugello racing
circuit in Italy to learn how to *really* drive the Testarossa. Just picture
yourself racing around the track at 120 mph while Guido, your instructor, barks at you in a thick Italian accent that you are not shifting at the

correct RPM or apexing your turns properly. Now that's real product training.

Summary

The key points to remember from this chapter include the following:

- Customer education is the process by which companies systematically share their knowledge and skills with external customers to foster the development of positive customer attitudes.
- There are three primary kinds of customers: buyers, users, and resellers.
- Customer education is a marketing tool that relates to the product and promotion components of the marketing mix.
- The three domains of learning are knowledge, skills, and attitudes.
- The process of education bridges the gap between customers and learning.
- From an organizational perspective, customer education is primarily aligned with sales and marketing.

Customer education is more than teaching customers how to use a product. It is a process that strives to build and maintain a relationship with customers by helping customers learn. As such, marketing is the heart of customer education—part of both the product itself and the promotion for the product.

Analyzing Performance Problems with Customers and Products

In any professional discipline, there are methods and models that guide work. Lawyers follow rules of law and court conduct in defending cases. Hotel chefs have specific processes for preparing large numbers of meals simultaneously for banquets. Molecular scientists use methods of good laboratory practice to ensure their experiments do not become contaminated.

Like these other professions, customer education practitioners have their own methods and models to ensure the integrity and consistency of results. The design of any quality educational solution has as its foundation the science of systems thinking, a means of analyzing and describing the whole of human action in the form of inputs, processing, and outputs. The manifestation of systems thinking for designing educational solutions is instructional systems design. (See Exhibit 3–1.) Instructional systems design starts with analysis, which is the focus of this chapter. Later chapters will address the other elements of the model.

Before designing and developing customer education solutions, you first need to be sure you are working on valid problems that you can solve with education. The heart of these problems is performance: the

Exhibit 3-1   Instructional Systems Design Model

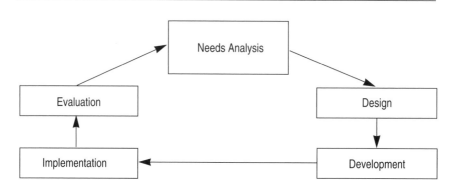

customers' ability to act in a way you or they desire. Customers may have problems acting in a desired way if:

- They do not have the appropriate knowledge or skill.
- The design of the product is so poor that they cannot figure it out.
- They do not have the motivation to understand the product or use it correctly.
- There are no incentives to stimulate the customer to act in a certain way.

Understanding these causes is important, because they will lead you to the most viable solution for the problem. For instance, customer education is only worthwhile if the causes reflect a lack of knowledge, skills, or motivation. Why? Because you can educate people to build their knowledge and to stimulate their motivation. However, education cannot fix a product design problem or provide a tangible incentive.

Gap analysis is a methodology for discovering solutions to a problem involving the actions of people. The purpose of gap analysis is to uncover the root cause of a problem by comparing an actual situation to a desired, or optimal, situation. Gap analysis is an important tool for customer educators, because customer education is not the right solution for every customer problem. Rather than teaching the customer, you might find that fixing the source of the problem, such as the ergonomic design of the product will solve the problem better, faster, and most cost-effectively. The process of analyzing customer performance problems will lead you to the best solution.

Customer Performance

When customers do not act as you desire them to, it is a performance problem. *Performance* describes specific actions that deliver a desired result. For example, when a customer buys your product, his or her performance is the act of buying, and the result is the exchange of goods for money. Similarly, when a customer assembles your product, assembly is the performance and a functioning product is the result. Performance capability is important to the customer, of course, but it will also affect the performance of the systems and processes within your company. Customers who maintain a product incorrectly might increase the quantity of calls or product returns to your company.

Assessing the performance of customers and your internal systems revolves around four basic measures: quality, quantity, time, and cost.[1]

- **Quality** relates to how well. A quality measure might include how well something works or the satisfaction one experiences from the result.
- **Quantity** relates to how much. The volume of product produced or the number of products sold are typical examples of quantity.
- **Time** relates to how fast or how slow. For instance, you might desire the customer to assemble a product in less than five minutes.
- **Cost** relates to how much money. Did the performance increase revenues and decrease costs, or vice versa?

Here is a scenario that shows how to assess customer problems and their effects on your company systems. You are facing an overburdened customer service department. Customer calls are coming in at a higher level than can be supported by the current staff. The lack of responsiveness and service is upsetting customers, and the overwork is burning out your staff and raising turnover.

You begin looking into the problem by analyzing the incoming calls. Here you notice that a large percentage of calls have to do with customers wanting information on how to clean the product. You also notice that there have been a number of product returns due to improper cleaning. You analyze these numbers against the number of products you have shipped and realize that 27 percent of the products shipped require some level of service to resolve cleaning problems. This information gives you a quality measure. Additionally, the number of calls and the number of product returns give you a quantity measure.

As you look into the call center database further, you notice that it takes on average 10 minutes to resolve a customer's cleaning problem. This is a time measure. To figure out why it takes so long, you listen to a couple of recorded service calls that deal with the cleaning problem. Here you discover that because cleaning requires disassembling certain components, customers want someone to hold their hand through the entire cleaning process, which takes 10-15 minutes.

With the information collected so far, you calculate the yearly cost of these problems. You multiply the number of calls by the average time per call. Next, you multiply this number by the per-minute telephone charges and the per-minute salary and benefits of a customer service rep. The out-of-pocket cost to help customers through this problem is a little over $100,000.

From this simple scenario, you can see how performance problems result in an increase in calls, an increase in time, and an increase in cost. By establishing benchmark measures, you will have the means to assess the effectiveness of the solutions you try.

CAUSES OF PERFORMANCE PROBLEMS

What prevents customers from achieving expected results time and time again? Research has shown that there are four primary factors that affect human performance: lack of knowledge or skill, flaws in the environment, lack of motivation, and lack of incentives.[2]

Lack of Knowledge or Skill. When customers lack knowledge or skill, they do not have the ability to perform. For instance, they may be unaware of your product—a lack of knowledge. Hence, they do not have the ability to buy. If a product is new to a customer, then it is likely that the customer has no idea of how to use it correctly—a potential lack of skill. People who rent cars are particularly at risk.[3] Although the basic elements of the car are known to them, such as steering wheel, gas pedal, and brake, specific controls that are different from their own car are a complete mystery. Adjusting the radio, turning on the lights or windshield wipers, even beeping the horn can be difficult. Customers lack knowledge of the new environment and the skills to operate within that environment. This lack of knowledge and skills ultimately affects their performance, accounting for the increased incidence of rental car accidents and damage.

New systems and technologies are a hotbed for gaps in knowledge and skills. Customers who face the daunting task of buying a computer for the first time experience a dizzying array of new terminology. RAM, ROM chips, processor speed, input device, pixels, hardware, software, floppies, and hard drives are all new concepts for the customer and must be learned before the customer can have both productive buying and using experiences.

Flaws in the Environment. Imagine a customer who is trying to assemble a product without the tools required to do the job correctly. Or, worse yet, a customer who is trying to use a software program that lacks any consistency or logic in its user interface. The customer might have the knowledge and skills to perform the task, yet there is something about the product that is inhibiting the customer's performance. There is a flaw in the environment.

Environmental elements that can contain flaws include processes, resources, people, and tools.[4] A *process* is a sequence of events or recipe. When followed, a process will result in a specific outcome. However, if a process is incorrect, then the customer will not achieve the result. For example, companies have processes for how they take orders from customers. The process typically involves understanding what the customer wants, resolving questions the customer has, making the exchange of money for goods, and delivering the product to the customer. If a key component of this process is broken, such as the inability to process credit cards, then the process fails and the expected result, a sale, does not happen.

Resources revolve around money and time. The amount of money you have to complete a task and the amount of time you have to do it can affect the end result, which can affect performance. For instance, you might want to design the most extensive customer education program ever devised for your product, yet the budget for the program is a mere $3,000. Additionally, you are given two weeks to produce it. The resources you are given cannot achieve your vision of the perfect program. Thus, you have to make do with what you have.

People are another factor that impacts performance. If a salesperson is rude to customers or a trainer treats customers like children in a kindergarten class, it will affect how customers perform. The same holds true for a trainer who cannot train effectively, since he or she will not be able to pass along the appropriate skills and knowledge to customers.

Many tasks require people to use tools in order to achieve desired results. *Tools* are devices that enable people to accomplish tasks. One form of tool is the hard tool. Hard tools are such things as screwdrivers, wrenches, saws, and hammers that enable customers to manipulate, assemble, or use products. Another form of tool is the soft tool. Soft tools can take the forms of a user interface for a software program or the buttons on a microwave oven that control time and temperature. Other examples of tools include typewriter keyboards, controls on your car radio, buttons on your phone, or the time-setting mechanism on a wristwatch.

Tools that are missing or poorly designed affect customer performance. If you sell a bed frame that uses special fastening devices but neglect to include the special tool that enables the customer to engage the fasteners, the customer will not be able to complete the task. Similarly, if the buttons that allow you to set your VCR are perplexing and difficult to use, then you will probably abandon the task and live with the VCR's clock blinking 12:00.

Lack of Motivation. There probably have been times in your life when you simply did not want to do what was expected. Maybe you drove 65 mph in a 55 mph zone or deliberately avoided completing an assignment. You might have had the knowledge and skills to accomplish the task and the environment was conducive to success, but you still did not perform. Why? Perhaps you did not have the motivation to perform.

Motivation reflects why a customer chooses to perform in a certain way. There are two kinds of motivation: intrinsic and extrinsic. *Intrinsic motivation* is when the customer's own needs, drives, and ambitions result in a specific level of performance. *Extrinsic motivation* is when an outside force, such as a reward, is offered for specific performance. Extrinsic motivation in the form of incentives is discussed in the next section. In this section, we will focus on intrinsic motivation.

Psychologist John Keller describes intrinsic motivation as the relationship between the value of the performance to the individual and the expectancy that the performance will result in success.[5] He expresses this relationship as a mathematical formula, whereby:

$$\text{Value} \times \text{Expectancy} = \text{Motivation}$$

If a customer believes that a specific performance is worthwhile and that his or her chances of success are high, then the customer's motivation to perform will be high. However, if the performance is not valued by the customer and he or she expects to fail, then motivation will be low.

What are the key sources of intrinsic motivation? Abraham Maslow's hierarchy of needs provides a general classification.[6] (See Exhibit 3–2.) Maslow's hierarchy is a classification of people's motives. At the bottom of the hierarchy, the needs for safety, shelter, and physiological well-being motivate people to look both ways before crossing a street, run to the basement when a tornado approaches, and to take a trip to the supermarket when hungry. In the middle of the hierarchy, needs for love, understanding, and being part of a group will motivate people to seek out relationships, engage in educational activities, and behave in a manner acceptable to peers. At the top of Maslow's scheme are the needs for aesthetics and self-actualization, which motivate people to seek consistency and order in their lives and to aspire to a state of mind in which they are at peace with themselves.

Lack of Incentives. Intrinsic motivation arises from within the customer whereas extrinsic motivation, in the form of incentives, comes from a source outside the customer. Consider, for example, your job. There are numerous incentives to encourage your performance, such as your salary and benefits, bonuses, recognition by your boss, and the threat of being fired.

The same holds true for customers. Your resellers, for instance, might only perform at high levels if you award prizes for sales volume. Employees of your customer might only use the new industrial

Exhibit 3–2   Maslow's Hierarchy of Needs

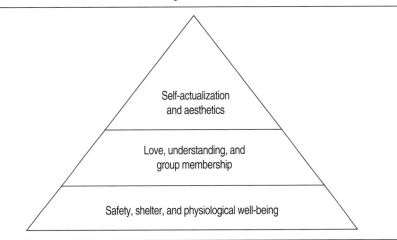

Self-actualization
and aesthetics

Love, understanding, and
group membership

Safety, shelter, and physiological well-being

Source: Adapted from E.R. Hilgard, R.L. Atkinson and R.C. Atkinson, *Introduction to Psychology*, 7th ed. (New York: Harcourt Brace Jovanovich, 1979).

equipment to its fullest potential if the company increases their hourly wage by 50 cents. You can train these customers to perform, and you can give these customers the tools to perform, but without an incentive, they will not perform.

Software companies are using an interesting practice of negative incentives to encourage customers to seek out solutions to their problems in manuals and other information sources: they charge for technical support. Whereas a positive incentive is when you give somebody a reward, a negative incentive is when you take something of value away. In this case, the negative incentive is the $1.50 per minute charge to speak to a technical support person.

THE RELATIONSHIP BETWEEN THE PERFORMANCE FACTORS

Customer education is only a solution for problems arising from the lack of knowledge and skills or motivation. Education can teach customers how to perform and can shape a customer's intrinsic motivators. Education cannot, however, change the environment customers work in nor provide incentives to stimulate performance. As such, it is often more desirable to fix the environment or offer an incentive to enable customers to succeed, rather than to throw education at the problem.

You can use education to overcome flaws in the environment and motivation, but the solution you develop will typically be wasteful and inappropriate. To illustrate this point. Donald Norman, author of *The Psychology of Everyday Things,* notes with some amusement the faucet situation at the Ranmoor dormitory, University of Sheffield. To use the faucets, guests must push down on them gently. However, one would never know this by looking at the faucet. So, after receiving one too many calls at the front desk for help, the dormitory management added faucet operation instructions to the information pamphlet given to guests. However, what guest would think to look there for instructions on using a faucet? Norman suggests that the instructions should have been put directly on the faucets, but advocates a more permanent solution—new faucets. "When simple things need instructions, it is a certain sign of poor design."[7]

Not everything is as simple as faucets. Early personal computers required customers to memorize numerous DOS commands, because these commands were not visible in the user interface. This meant that it took customers a long time to reach competency, which reduced productivity.

To overcome the problem of the poor user interface of their operating systems (an environmental flaw), computer companies threw education at the problem. The first DOS computer came with three thick user manuals. Did the manuals help? Customers with high intrinsic motivation were able to muddle through the manuals and learn the system. However, time and its related consequences were the price to pay. Customers without the motivation to stick with the manuals faired worse. They did not achieve the performance they desired and eventually abandoned using the computer.

In 1984, the first commercial graphic user interface found its way to customers on the Macintosh computer. Ten years later, every personal computer sold comes with a graphic user interface, either the Macintosh operating system or Microsoft's Windows. The result? Customer productivity improved. It is now faster to learn to use a computer than ever before. Instead of having to recall arcane names and commands to get work done, customers click on icons and select commands from menus. Making these controls visible to the user at all times saved the customer from tedious memorization and laborious recall. It turned using the computer from a recall task to a recognition task, which is infinitely easier for the human mind to learn.

Now that the environment had changed, something else changed as well. User manuals got smaller. For example, Apple's line of PowerPC computers comes with one, slim volume. In this case, the improved environment (user interface) makes the system easier to learn without relying on manuals and other teaching solutions.

An acquaintance from Sun Microsystems who works in user education believes that the role of anyone involved in customer education is to make the job obsolete. This is truly a lofty goal, but the essence of the statement is that customer educators should look for ways to simplify the environment in which the customer will work. Doing so will make products easier to understand and use, simplifying the customers' task immensely.

As illustrated by these situations, the resolution of customer problems is rarely fixed by the addition of instructions or a change in the environment. Rather, the best solution typically comes from orchestrating strategies that address each of the four factors of performance: knowledge and skills, environment, motivation, and incentive. Analyzing customer performance problems through the process of gap analysis leads you to understand how the four factors affect the system you are trying to change. With this knowledge, you will not use education where it does not belong.

Analyzing Performance Problems

Gap analysis is a method for identifying and prioritizing needs. Its power comes from a relatively simple model. (See Exhibit 3–3.) The process of gap analysis begins when you sense there is a problem: customers are not performing as expected. To define the problem, you compare the current state of things, *what is,* to the desired state of things, *what should be.* Another way of thinking about this is comparing *actuals* to *optimals.*[8] The difference between these two elements is the gap, which is also referred to as a need. What flows from the gap are causes: the forces that contribute to the formation of the gap. Causes include the lack of knowledge or skills, flaws in the environment, lack of motivation, or lack of incentives.

Not only does the gap analysis model help you identify needs, but it also helps you uncover which needs are more important than others. Through gap analysis, you break down needs into their core components. This enables you to clearly compare the significance of each need and the relative resources required to resolve each need. These two factors help you plan which needs to resolve first.

ENTRY INTO THE MODEL

Entry into the model begins with what Roger Kaufman, professor at Florida State University, calls *need sensing.*[9] In a person's everyday work, there is a continual sensing of possible problems. For instance, you might notice a rash of phone calls to your 800-number, hear an

Exhibit 3-3   Gap Analysis Model

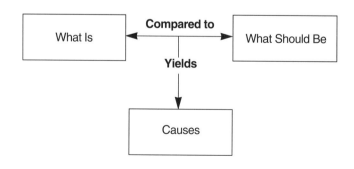

anecdote about a customer's problems with a product, or read an article in a business magazine featuring the problems of a competitor or a business in a related industry. There are four good places to look for the kinds of problems for which customer education can offer a solution: product, customer, competition, and company.

- **Product.** You can identify problems by knowing the strengths and weaknesses of your product in terms of ergonomics, usability, and terminology. Involvement with the product development team is imperative for customer educators.
- **Customer.** The demographics of your customers, their education levels, and their prior experience with a product class can offer clues about whether they will have problems with the product. Additionally, customers' reaction to the product, through customer service data, will also alert you to problems.
- **Competition.** Knowing the products of your competition as well as the customer education solutions they offer can reveal problems with your own products and customer education.
- **Company.** Internal resources and politics can cause problems that ultimately affect the customer. However, the company also provides the leadership, vision, and mission that serve as criteria by which you can judge the severity of problems.

Through these various sources you will either predict problems before they occur or react to problems once they have happened. Thus, need sensing can be predictive or reactionary.

Predictive Need Sensing. Predictive need sensing is when you identify problems before a product gets into customers' hands. The product development process is an excellent source for identifying potential problems. During this process, a product team might hit barriers in product development: unavailable technology, a tight development schedule, or a lack of agreement between team members about the "right" solution. One team of which I was a member had a catch phrase, Not for March,™ used whenever someone introduced a new idea or feature. It meant that the idea or feature would not be part of the first version of the product, scheduled for March. Because of these barriers, elements of the product that impact customer performance might be left out.

Product development teams will themselves notice the relative ease or difficulty of specific product features. To leverage this knowledge into practical solutions, I strongly encourage that a technical writer or instructional designer be part of the product team from day one. There is no time like the present to begin figuring out how you will teach a customer a new product.

Another source of predictive need sensing is your own intuition. If you find a product difficult to understand or use, then chances are that customers will have the same reaction. Another big indicator is when you observe an "expert" with the product make mistakes when he or she demonstrates it to you or prefaces the demonstration with a 30-minute explanation. Obviously, something is wrong.

Market research, including such activities as user testing and focus groups, can also provide predictive data regarding needs. Putting the product, instructions and all, into the hands of customers (along with a well-designed research methodology) can yield interesting results. AT&T did this with a two-year "secret" trial of its new interactive television multimedia system. In this trial, AT&T recruited 50 homes of AT&T employees as users. While computers tracked every click of the remote controls, people used the system. They watched TV programs, played interactive game shows, and participated in educational programs, such as Clickety Corners, a spelling tutor. Periodic focus groups allowed the users to talk about their experiences. One research finding related to how users learned to use the system. Vince Grosso, who headed the project, says that success in getting people to use the system related to making it as easy as TV, not as difficult as a computer. In come cases, Grosso found children teaching their parents to use the system. As a result of this study, AT&T focused on making the system simple. This even included getting rid of the instruction manual.[10]

Reactive Need Sensing.   Reactive need sensing occurs when products are in the hands of customers. As customers use a product, they might find they cannot do something, so they contact you by phone, letter, or in person to complain and resolve their problem. When this happens, there is an obvious need.

The channels of communication you have open to customers, combined with the strength of your information management systems and reporting capabilities, are critical factors in reactive need sensing. Customers need to be aware of how to contact your company's sales reps, trainers, or service technicians. That is why 800-numbers are often printed on products. Companies want customers to call about even the slightest problem.

The data that companies collect from these calls must be accessible by customer educators. The database must be organized so that they can generate periodic quantitative reports as well as easily prepare future queries. Good databases allow customer service specialists to code problems and their resolutions. For instance, if customers keep calling about a problem that is clearly explained in the user manual, then perhaps the instructions are not featured prominently enough in the manual. Having this type of information coded in the database and printed in weekly reports is extremely useful. It will gauge severity and point you in the direction of a solution.

One chemical manufacturer has a complete system in place to identify, prioritize, and resolve reactive needs. Due to the wide range of possible experiments and the innovative uses of chemicals, it is impossible to predict the problems customers might encounter. Thus, the company has a process culminating with the publication of a user bulletin to react to problems when they occur. If a customer calls the company with a problem, the call is forwarded to the company's core lab facility, an in-house research facility. There, an expert with the chemical works with the customer to resolve the problem. If the resolution would apply to a wide number of customers, as assessed by other customer calls and the nature of the problem, then the scientist and a technical writer develop a user bulletin that explains the problem and documents a solution. The company publishes the user bulletin and distributes it to other customers. For problems that are severe, the company has gone as far as producing videotapes that demonstrate how customers can resolve problems.

DEFINING WHAT IS

When your predictive or reactive need sensing activities reveal a performance problem, your first step in the gap analysis process is to capture the essence of the situation in writing. To do this, take a mental snapshot of the problem. The snapshot you take must show what is happening now, in the present. What are customers doing? How are they failing? How do you know?

The problem statement should be, above all, performance-based. Performance-based statements require a clear, specific description of the customer's behavior, a measure attesting to the degree of the problem, and any conditions that are relevant. These statements focus on what the customer is doing, not how the customer is doing it.

Exhibit 3–4 shows examples of performance-based and non–performance-based statements. The first example illustrates a predictive need. The statement hypothesizes what will happen when customers get their hands on a piece of software. The measure, "90 percent of customers," might be speculative, or it can be derived from research activities, such as user testing. The contrasting statement tells what customers will not be able to do, but it lacks measures and specificity. The second example shows a reactive need. The behavior is "assemble the product," and the measures are "90 percent of our customers" and "three hours." Compare this with the statement that is not performance-based. It describes how customers are failing, rather than what the failure is. It does not contain any form of measure. Performance-based statements obviously require some thinking and research. This is where data from product teams, market research, and in-house customer information databases becomes useful. By quantifying the what is statement, you provide proof that it is authentic. You also provide a benchmark by which to measure future solutions.

Also be aware that your what is statement should get at the heart of the problem. If your statements are too broad, it will be difficult to pin down the causes of the problem. To make a problem statement useful, try to find at least three or four reasons that have specific measures associated with them. If these reasons still seem too broad, refine them again until the statements define specific, manageable problems.

Exhibit 3-4   What Is Statements: Performance-Based and Not Performance-Based

Performance-Based	Not Performance-Based
90% of customers will not be able to complete sample setup for multiple probe experiments unless they call technical support one time.	Customer will not be able to figure out the sample setup interface.
90% of our customers take more than three hours to assemble the storage shed.	Customers keep breaking screws.

WHAT SHOULD BE

The statement that complements *what is* and completes the definition of the gap is *what should be*. This statement, which is also performance-based, describes a goal or target that, if achieved, typifies success. Whereas what is is a snapshot of the present, what should be is a look into the future. It is the ideal to which all of your solutions must aspire.

Four interrelated factors guide the definition of what should be:

- Customer expectations and requirements
- Product technology
- Competition
- Profitability

The customers' expectations and requirements describe what performance customers want products to provide. For example, cars should always start on the first turn of the key, Minute Rice should cook in one minute, one can of Scotch-Guard should cover 20 square feet, and a fast-food meal for four should cost under $20. Reliability, speed, accuracy, and cost are principal performance measures to look for when trying to quantify customer expectations and requirements.

Customers might expect a lot, but their expectations are often balanced with the product's technology. Sometimes technology will enable you to meet or exceed customer expectations. Sometimes it will not. For instance, customers have always expected an easy-to-use personal computer, even back in 1980. Yet the technology to support a graphical user interface was not available. Thus, customers were stuck with a poor user interface and lots of user manuals. On the other hand, technology can occasionally surprise customers. Automated credit card processors on gas station pumps surprised many customers by reducing the time it takes to pay for gas.

Knowing what the competition is doing is always an important factor. Consider one of Apple Computer's advertising campaigns. It compared the steps and time required to set up a Macintosh to a Windows-compatible computer. Obviously, the Macintosh was far easier to set up. If a competitor starts doing things that affect customer performance, what will you do to keep up or move ahead?

If the plan to improve customer performance will not contribute to making a profit, then it is not worth doing. Profitability is a strong regulating factor in decision making. In the 1980s, several videocassette recorder companies included instructional videotapes to show customers how to use the equipment. However, this was at a time when the cost of VCRs was coming down and margins were being squeezed. The instructional videos did not stimulate breakthrough performance by customers, and the cost of the videos impeded margins. Ultimately, they were dropped.

Writing a what should be statement requires you to balance and synthesize these four interrelated factors. If customers want to be able to assemble the product in less than 10 minutes, can your product's technology support such a requirement? What if a competitor's product takes only seven minutes to assemble? Does your product need to match this performance? Are calls to customer service blowing your profit margin? Market research data, interviews with product managers, engineers, and designers, a library of your competitor's products, and cost and pricing data should provide the information you need to define what should be.

Exhibit 3–5 shows the what is statements from Exhibit 3-4 with their corresponding what should be statements. In the first example, the what should be statement reflects that the customer expects this task to be easy and predicts that the product's technology can support a 95 percent success rate. The same rationale holds true for the second example, except that the competition's product takes 90 minutes to assemble. Here, quick assembly time will prove to be a competitive advantage.

As you generate what should be statements to complement what is statements, pay attention to the scope of the need. Is it just one perfectionist who cannot achieve the performance he or she expects, or are

Exhibit 3–5 What Is and What Should Be Statements

What Is	What Should Be
90% of customers will not be able to complete sample setup for multiple probe experiments unless they call technical support one time.	95% of customers can set up a multiple probe experiment without contacting technical support.
90% of our customers take more than three hours to assemble the storage shed.	100% of our customers can assemble the storage shed in less than one hour.

problems experienced by a few customers the first drip of a dam that is about to burst? Focus on the needs that offer the greatest value for the least cost.

CAUSES

By defining what is and what should be, you have established the boundaries of your problem. But what is causing the problem? Now it is time for you to play detective and begin asking why? Why are customers failing? Why are so many support calls coming in? Why does it take 90 percent of our customers longer than three hours to assemble the product?

As discussed earlier, the causes you identify will filter into the four factors of performance: knowledge and skills, environment, motivation, and incentives. Those causes that fall into the knowledge and skills or motivation categories will eventually lead to customer education solutions. Those causes dealing with environment or incentives will require a different course of action. The appropriateness of your solution hinges on how well you flush out the causes.

Identifying causes requires an in-depth investigation into the problem. The data you collected when you originally defined the problems will again be useful in your search for causes. You can sift this data to draw conclusions about the causes of customer performance or collect new data if the existing data is insufficient. The general rule of drawing conclusions from the data is that of triangulation. Triangulation is seeking at least three data points that confirm a conclusion. For example, if a design engineer confides that a particular product feature will be difficult to use, user tests of the product feature prove that customers do have difficulty, and technical writers have problems writing clear instructions for the feature, then it is safe to conclude that a primary cause of the problem is environmental. Your conclusion is based on the consistency of the three sources. The following examples show how causes are derived from a performance problem.

Example 1: A Predictive Need. The first example, Exhibit 3–6, shows the results of a cause analysis for the sample setup problem. The customer educator worked closely with the product development team throughout the product development process to completely understand the product of interest, which is a software application for conducting scientific experiments. In addition to this knowledge, the customer educator interviewed and observed in-house scientists as they used prototypes of the system. These scientists also worked closely with customers in test sites and were able to funnel their comments back to the product team.

One conclusion the customer educator reached was fairly obvious: the system automated and improved an experiment that had always been done by hand. Thus, there was a knowledge and skills gap in customers knowing what the system was, what it could do, and how to use it. Customers had never experienced such a system.

A second conclusion revolved around a key feature of the software that dealt with how the user would specify the samples in their experiment. Because the science for the system was not quite resolved when development of the software began, the team developed a solution. As

Exhibit 3-6   Results of a Cause Analysis for a Software Application

What Is	What Should Be
90% of customers will not be able to complete sample setup for mutliple probe experiments unless they call technical support one time.	95% of customers can set up a multiple probe experiment without contacting technical support.

Causes

Knowledge/Skills	Environment	Motivation	Incentive
• Users are not aware of the nomenclature and procedure for sample setup.	• Many users do not know the sample sheet is a three-dimensional matrix, because only two dimensions are visible at a time. • The three-dimensional sample sheet is not consistent with how users think about analyzing their samples.	• Not a problem. The equipment is expensive, the cost of failed experiments is high, and task is part of a user's job, so we expect a user to be highly motivated to resolve the problem independenly.	• Technical support is free for the first year of product ownership. Thus, there is no incentive for the user not to call.

experience with the science grew, it became clear to team members, scientists, and customers that the sample setup solution did not map well to how users thought of their sample setup. Observations of users found a high level of difficulty in completing the setup. Technical writers complained about how they would explain the setup. From these perspectives, the customer educator concluded that fixing the user interface of the software would undoubtedly resolve most of these problems.

Another conclusion related to customers' motivation. In this case, there was no reason to believe that customers would not be motivated to successfully use the system. The demographics showed that lab technicians working for principal investigators would be the primary users of the system. Thus, the fact that users' jobs depended on their successfully using the system indicated a high source of motivation. Additionally, the high cost of the system as well as the high cost of materials motivate customers to learn the setup procedures. In this market, failures can be expensive. Motivation was not an issue in resolving the performance problem.

The last conclusion focused on incentives. There were no incentives to perform or not perform. Customer calls to technical support were free for the first year of product ownership. The company's service philosophy and product pricing was so entrenched that charging customers for technical support calls was out of the question. Customers expected this level of service for the investment they were making.

Example 2: Reaction to Customer Difficulties. The product in this example is a prefabricated storage shed. Customers erect them in their yards to provide additional storage space for garden tools, equipment, and general household clutter. The problem was prompted by a rash of angry letters to the company by customers who had extraordinary difficulty erecting the shed. A subsequent survey confirmed this and contributed to the what is statement. Exhibit 3–7 shows the results of the analysis that define the problem and its causes.

Most of the causes identified by the customer educator who analyzed this situation came from pretending to be a customer and trying to assemble the product personally. From a knowledge and skills standpoint, the instructions that came with the product were originally written for a previous version and had never been fully updated. It was reasonable to conclude that given the state of the instructions, customers had difficulty learning how to complete the task.

Another factor that amazed the customer educator was the array of tools needed to assemble the structure. No fewer that three different

Exhibit 3–7   Results of a Cause Analysis for a Storage Shed

What Is	What Should Be
90% of our customers take more than three hours to assemble the storage shed.	100% of our customers can assemble the storage shed in less than one hour.

Causes

Knowledge/Skills	Environment	Motivation	Incentive
• Product instructions poorly describe the assembly procedure. • There is no customer support number for customers to call. • Resellers are not trained in product assembly so they cannot be of assistance to customers.	• Assembly hardware is not standardized, requiring the customer to use several kinds of tools to complete assembly. • 30% of product pieces were predrilled incorrectly, requiring customers to redrill holes.	• Not a problem. Customers are buying the storage shed to clean clutter out of their garages and homes.	• None offered.

types of screwdrivers and three different wrench sizes were required for the job. Additional tools would make the job even easier. Coupled with this were the defects in the parts. Predrilled holes were out of place, causing parts not to line up correctly. Further investigation into manufacturing processes and quality control found that 30 percent of the pieces going out were predrilled incorrectly.

Even with these failures, customers had no one to call for help. The company did not publish its phone number on the product. (It did not have the resources to deal with end-user calls. Rather, it relied on the resellers to handle customer problems.) However, further inquiry with salespeople and resellers showed that no one taught resellers how to assemble the product, or even how to deal with customer problems.

Customer surveys showed that they were extremely motivated to get the shed built. Typically, their impetus for buying the shed was to have another place to store the stuff piling up in the garage. One customer wrote on the survey that if he did not get the shed built and get his stuff organized, his wife would leave him.

Summary

The concepts to remember from this chapter include the following:

- The primary means of analyzing customer performance problems is a gap analysis, which compares what the customer is doing to what the customer should be doing.
- The four causes of customer performance problems are lack of knowledge or skills, flaws in the environment, lack of motivation, and lack of incentive.
- The four places one should analyze to uncover performance problems are product, customer, competition, and company.
- The two kinds of need sensing are predictive and reactive.

Knowing why customers do not perform is the first step in building a customer education strategy. To develop the best solution for the problem, it is important to identify whether causes reflect a lack of knowledge or skills, a flaw in the environment, the lack of motivation, or a lack of incentive. Choosing a customer education strategy for a problem whose cause is environmental is destined for failure. There is just no way to train a customer to turn a product on if there is no on switch.

What does this mean for the customer educator? It means going beyond the boundaries of training in order to develop practical, lasting solutions to customer performance problems. Customer educators need to be involved in product design to help predict the difficulties customers will face and provide a voice to help negotiate solutions to those problems. Customer educators need to be involved in analyzing customer feedback to help identify problems and recommend solutions to those problems.

Customer performance is the measure by which customer educators assess their worth to the organization. If customer performance is affected by factors other than training, then customer educators should have the encouragement, skills, and opportunity to make contributions in other areas that have an effect on customer performance.

Driving Forces for Customer Education

Customer problems can stimulate big ideas. Ask anyone who works on the frontlines with customers: salespeople, customer service reps, or technical support specialists. They will tell you why the customer is having problems, and they will recommend inspiring solutions to those problems: "Customers need a videotape to show them exactly how to complete the process," intones a technical support specialist. "If only we could develop a course to teach customers how to work with us," mentions an inside sales rep. Unfortunately, people often lose sight of the relative importance of the problems stimulating their ideas. A company might spend 80 percent of its customer education time and resources designing a solution that accounts for 20 percent of the desired results. What is needed is a way to gauge the relative importance of customer performance problems to ensure that ideas and solutions contribute to meaningful results.

Driving forces are a means to assess the relative importance of problems. The principle of driving forces was first articulated in the 1930s by Kurt Lewin, the father of modern social psychology, as part of his force-field theory. Lewin's theory postulated that systems are held in equilibrium by forces wanting change (driving forces), and forces resisting change (restraining forces). Change can happen only when the relative strength of the driving forces outweighs the relative strength of the restraining forces.[1]

Knowledge, skills, and attitude gaps quickly come to mind as the predominant driving forces for adopting customer education. But, in a business setting, you could never convince anyone to invest in a customer education program just because customers have a knowledge gap. Why? Because you have not articulated the return on investment. Decision makers need to know whether closing the knowledge gap will make customers buy more product. Will it reduce costs? Will it eliminate litigation? Will it keep customers happy and satisfied? Will it build customer relationships?

Typical driving forces for customer education align themselves into three categories: marketing, legal, and operational. Marketing forces relate to stimulating demand for product. Legal forces relate to product liability and compliance with regulations. Operational forces relate to reducing costs and leveraging the knowledge that exists within the organization.

Marketing Forces

Customer education can cause more people to want to do business with your company and buy your products. By ensuring that customers have sufficient knowledge about your products and are satisfied with them, you will find new customers, open new markets, and retain existing customers.

INCREASING CUSTOMER SATISFACTION

Organizations satisfy customers when the perceived performance of a product (including the product itself and activities surrounding acquisition and use of the product) is greater than or equal to the customer's expectations. There is probably no bigger buzzword in marketing than customer satisfaction, because customer satisfaction has a positive correlation with profitability. The more satisfied customers are, the more business they will do with a company. The insurance industry encourages agents to educate their clients in areas such as defining one's needs or choosing the best coverage to address those needs. In this setting, the path to customer satisfaction is a one-on-one education session between the agent and the client.[2] Customer education also produces other outcomes associated with customer satisfaction: reduced complaints, customer loyalty, and positive word-of-mouth promotion.

Reduced Complaints. If a customer has the knowledge and skills to successfully use a product, then the customer has nothing to complain about. However, three situations can turn any customer into a complainer:

- Misusing products, such as using garden shears to cut sheet metal.
- Failing to maintain products, such as not adding oil to a car.
- Buying the wrong product for an intended purpose, such as buying a PH1A oil filter instead of a PH3B oil filter.

Training magazine editor Bob Filipczak estimates that one-third of all customer complaints are from customers who do not know how to use a product.[3] Customer satisfaction advocates argue that it is the manufacturer's responsibility to make the use and care of products easy to understand. Reducing customer complaints will naturally increase customer satisfaction.

Customer Loyalty. If customers are successful in using a product, it is likely that they will continue to buy the product or patronize the company that sold them the product. The Technical Assistance Research Programs (TARP) conducted a number of studies in 1983 that investigated customer education and consumer loyalty. In one study, American Express prepared a booklet called "Mail Order Rights." Of the customers who read the booklet, 23 percent said it increased their confidence in American Express. Another study reviewed Coca Cola's booklet "How to Talk to a Company and Get Action." Of the customers who read it, 50 percent felt more confident about the company, and 15 percent said they would buy more Coca Cola products. In addition, 88 percent saved the booklet for future reference. One can interpret these results as evidence of increased customer loyalty.[4]

Loyalty among customers is difficult to develop: it is fragile and elusive, and it must be continually won and re-won.[5] Customers are not necessarily loyal to products or suppliers. Rather, they are loyal to the value resulting in the greatest satisfaction.[6] The old marketing adage is that it is more expensive to get new customers than to keep existing customers. Thus, organizations must consider how to keep their customers loyal.

A company's failure to maintain contact with a customer or provide new ideas and knowledge can result in "account churning," the turnover of customers due to neglect. This phenomenon is often the result of salespeople meeting targets and quotas—they get complacent when business is going well. The ongoing responsibility of customer education can help the sales force maintain business relationships. Keeping the customer informed about new methods, techniques, and ideas that are beneficial to their business is often a simple but effective strategy of building customer loyalty.

Customer service advocate Ron Zemke reports that of all the reasons for consumer buying behavior, trust is at the top of the list. Customers who are knowledgeable about a company's products and services and experienced with the company's systems for rectifying complaints and solving problems trust the company. Customer education can build a customer's knowledge to facilitate the development of trust.

Positive Word-of-Mouth Promotion. A customer who knows about a product and can successfully use the product will tell others of his or her satisfaction. Friends, acquaintances, and relatives are the most frequent sources of this word-of-mouth promotion. Word-of-mouth usually has positive connotations, but it can also be negative. Customers complain to other customers about products not working as expected, frequent breakdown and repairs, and bad service. Charles Carr, in his book *Frontline Customer Service,* estimates that 90 percent of dissatisfied customers will tell nine other people about the dissatisfaction, and 13 percent will tell 20 or more people.[7] The percentage of satisfied customers telling others about their satisfaction is significantly lower. Unfortunately, bad news travels fast.

The goal of customer education is to reduce negative word-of-mouth and increase positive word-of-mouth. Customer education programs can reduce complaints, eliminating the catalyst for negative word-of-mouth. Teaching customers to be successful with a product increases positive word-of-mouth. For example, in the American Express and Coca Cola studies described above, 50 percent of the booklet readers told at least two people about the information they had learned.

The traditional innovation adoption curve illustrates the importance of positive word-of-mouth. (See Exhibit 4–1.) Late adopters base their

Exhibit 4-1   Adoption of Innovations Curve

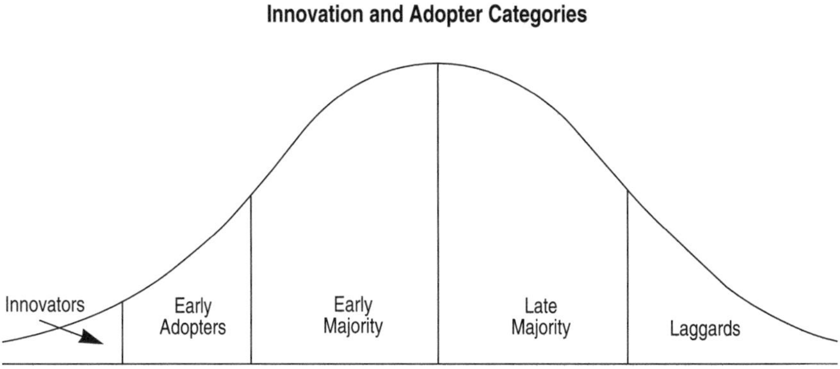

Innovation and Adopter Categories

| Innovators | Early Adopters | Early Majority | Late Majority | Laggards |

Source: Adapted from E.M. Rogers, *Diffusion of Innovations*, 3rd ed. (New York: The Free Press,

adoption choice on interpersonal communication and recommendation from early adopters. Therefore, it is important to satisfy early adopters so they communicate positive word-of-mouth to the late adopters.[8] Customer education is a method to facilitate positive communication.

STIMULATING DEMAND FOR PRODUCTS

A customer education program can help you tap new markets and new customers. It can also increase the profitability of existing markets. There are three models of how customer education can stimulate demand: how to do, how it works, and how to buy.

How to Do Model. In this model, a company teaches customers a skill that will stimulate their need to buy the company's products. The best example of this is the ski school at a ski area. The ski area cannot survive or grow unless it continuously has new skiers who can use the service it provides. The ski school, therefore, is an integral part of ensuring the success of the entire ski area. The more people it teaches to ski, the more people there are to provide a consistent, ongoing source of revenue to the ski area. The idea of a ski school crosses into other industries, such as investing.

People will not use investment services if they do not know how to invest. Thus, investment services companies must teach potential customers how to invest as a means to develop new business. Charles Schwab & Co. offers a whole range of educational materials on topics such as equities, bonds, mutual funds, and making investment decisions. First American Discount Corporation, which deals with more complex investments, such as commodities trading, also uses customer education to develop new customers. Its television advertisements promote a free dictionary of trading terms. This is followed by newsletters and other educational solutions intended to give customers sufficient knowledge about commodities trading so that they will begin to use First American's services in order to make trades.

The how to do model is not static. That is, you cannot offer classes for beginners only; rather customer education must continually meet the expanding needs of the customer. This will keep customers coming back to your place of business. Home Depot offers many how-to courses on home improvement and repair. The stores have a repeating, weekly curriculum that covers everything from refurbishing plumbing systems to installing new bathroom tile. Saturn automobile dealerships have a similar program. They invite Saturn owners into their dealerships for workshops on auto maintenance. In both these cases, the offer of how-to knowledge keeps people coming through the door and begins establishing a relationship between company and customer.

For industrial and business-to-business marketing, the how to do model relates more to teaching customers new processes or methods of business that will stimulate demand for products. Perkin-Elmer's Applied Biosystems Division must ensure customers know how to do Taqman PCR (a method of amplifying DNA) before those customers will be interested in using Perkin-Elmer's instruments and chemicals.

How It Works Model. The how it works model is another means for stimulating demand through customer education. Buying decisions are often dependent on the customer's knowledge of and skill with a product. The task of educating customers before the sale often falls to salespeople. Promotional materials supplement the salesperson's pitch by providing a concrete reminder of the product's features and benefits.

At computer shows and conferences, software manufacturers such as Microsoft, Aldus, and Claris hold training sessions in their booths on the exposition floor. In these hands-on sessions, customers learn product features and procedures for accomplishing tasks. One goal of these sessions is to give non-users a taste of the product. Another goal is to give existing users additional knowledge and skills so they will remain loyal to the product. This ensures subsequent purchase of product upgrades.

How to Buy Model. A third model for stimulating customer demand is the how to buy model. If customers have no experience with making purchase decisions for a certain class of product, then they are less likely to buy. For example, the Gibson Guitar Company was worried that customers did not know how to buy its electric guitars. Instead of advertising the strengths and weaknesses of its products, Gibson promoted its booklet, "How to Buy an Electric Guitar." The booklet advised customers on the criteria for evaluating electric guitars. (Which, of course, Gibson Guitars met with flying colors.)

DIFFERENTIATING YOUR PRODUCT FROM THE COMPETITION

Marketers are always looking for ways to make their product different from that of a competitor. Differentiation gives them an advantage in meeting the needs of customers, especially if customers value the features that make the product different. The concept of the value-added or whole product helps marketers make their product more than a commodity.

To better understand customer education's competitive role, consider these hypothetical examples of two competing commodity products, baking flour A and baking flour B. The product manager for flour A wants to grab market share from flour B. After reviewing market research data, he theorizes that if he teachers customers how to use flour A in new and interesting ways, more customers will buy flour A than flour B. Satisfied with this analysis, he develops a one-page package insert of innovative flour recipes and puts it in every package of flour A.

The product manager for flour B, ever on the alert, immediately spots flour A's new strategy. She assembles her product team to discuss how to respond to this new competitive challenge. The following options flow from the meeting: do nothing, do a similar insert, or do something better than a one-page insert, such as a free cookbook full of recipes using flour.

This example illustrates the two roles customer education plays in competition. In the first role, a company uses customer education to respond to customers' needs better than the competition, thus differentiating the product. Businessland, the computer retailer, differentiated itself from the competition by emphasizing customer education and service rather than price.

Corporate customers recognized this value, because computers are worthless unless employees know how to use them. Businessland attributed much of its growth and profitability to this strategy.

In the second role, competition can cause a company to match or surpass the competitor's activities. Many customers demand product training. Thus, nearly all companies offer it. The point of differentiation is quality. As companies add quality to their customer education, competitors often follow suit. Consider, for instance, IBM's HelpWare™ for its personal computer products. HelpWare is a high-quality, integrated customer education system combining self-instructional materials, training centers, and 800-number telephone support. It is likely that IBM's HelpWare is a response to the quality customer education offered by Compaq, Dell, and Apple.

The value of customer education as a competitive advantage is more noticeable now that product reviewers in trade and specialty magazines use it as a criteria in their product evaluations. Consider these two reviews in the same article in *CD-ROM World* magazine for competing computer systems:[9]

- For a Zeos International Computer: The Getting Started and User's Guides provide all the help you need to get up and running.
- For a USA Flex Computer: USA Flex computers do not include pretty system documentation booklets. In fact, if you've never set up a computer before, you may find yourself frustrated as you unwrap your new toy.

Customers do notice when customer education adds value to your product. Thus, it can be a useful strategy for differentiating your product from your competitor's product.

CORRECTING CONSUMER MISCONCEPTIONS

In a media-rich society, advertisements, editorials, television, radio, newspaper, telephone, fax, etc., bombard customers with information. Messages are normally accurate, but some messages disseminate misleading information. Controversial issues are enticing to the media, especially when the issues involve large corporations. Even though the media operate under a system of checks and balances, disinformation and one-sided perspective spread like wildfire, causing confusion and dissonance among consumers. NBC television's report of the exploding General Motors pickup truck is just one example of this media phenomenon.

Public relations strategists use customer education as a tool to combat misinformation. Whereas the case of General Motors was atoned for in public announcements in the media, the case of Equifax, one the nation's largest consumer credit agencies, shows how a more integrated customer education strategy helped overcome the negative publicity associated with its services.

Equifax suffered from an industry-wide media lashing regarding consumers' privacy. Consumer advocates charged that credit reporting firms disregarded the privacy of individuals whose credit records they possessed. In addition to disregarding privacy, the media accused the industry of sloppy recordkeeping and lax security. Equifax believed that these misconceptions and negative images could adversely affect its business. To correct this problem, Equifax turned to customer education.

Equifax produced several publications about how the credit reporting industry operates. It launched an advertising campaign to explain consumers' rights under the Fair Credit Reporting Act. Furthermore, it established an 800-number staffed 24 hours a day, seven days a week, to provide consumers with information about credit reporting. It is estimated that these programs cost $5 million per year.[10] By not responding to consumer misconceptions, you run many risks. Your company's image could lose value and become damaged beyond repair. The perceived quality of your products could become tarnished. Worst of all, you could lose customers.

Legal Forces

Legal forces are another driving force for customer education. Ensuring that your products carry the correct warnings and instructions can help reduce exposure to product liability suits. Providing customer education that complies with government legislation can avoid fines. Tailoring customer education to meet the requirements of industry organizations will not only avoid fines and sanctions from these organizations, but also qualify you to bid on major projects.

LIMITING PRODUCT LIABILITY

Lawn mowers, chain saws, automatic garage-door openers, paper-cutting machines, antennas, and hair dryers are but a few of the inherently dangerous products in common use. Uneducated customers run the risk of serious injury or death when using these types of products. Customers have the right to be informed about the products and services they use. According to Sam Brown, author of *The Product Liability Handbook,* the goal is to provide the customer with enough information to assemble, install, test, and use the product safety.[11]

Genie's customer education campaign illustrates one company's efforts to reduce the dangers associated with its automatic garage-door openers. Even though most automatic garage-door openers have safety features, such as automatic reversing mechanisms, accidents still occur. Children play games with automatic doors, pushing the door control button from inside the garage and trying to run outside before the door closes. Adults and children blindly open and close the automatic doors without checking for obstructions.

Over an eight-year period, automatic garage-door openers killed 45 children. Each year, automatic garage doors injure 2,000 children. In light of these figures, Genie president John Gray, quoted in the *Public Relations Journal,* stated, "Even one child's death is too many as far as I'm concerned. We saw this [accidents with automatic garage doors] as a potentially explosive issue and wanted to take a proactive approach to address an industry problem which we felt was not being addressed."[12] Genie analyzed customer service calls to discover the root causes of accidents. First, it found that customers did not perform the recommended garage-door opener maintenance. Second, customers were not aware of the dangers garage-door openers posed to children. To provide a solution, Genie designed a multifaceted customer education program:

- A safety brochure entitled "Don't Close the Door on Safety." The brochure contained tips for safe operation, maintenance, and testing of garage-door openers. The brochure also folded out into a poster.
- A publicity campaign promoting the brochure. Genie distributed a press kit containing the brochure, a news release, and a photo of a safety test to major newspapers.
- A series of articles by a Genie engineer. Genie distributed these articles to weekly newspapers around the country.
- An information kit for dealers and retailers.

- Safety-related advertisements in newspapers and magazines.

The results of Genie's customer education program are impressive. Genie estimates that 67 million people received the safety message. More than 30,000 brochures were distributed. School officials asked Genie employees to speak at school safety presentations. Additionally, Genie was able to position the company as one concerned about its products and their safe use.[13]

Educating and training customers to use products safely is a primary function of customer education. Ensuring the customer's safety is ethical. Moreover, courts can hold organizations liable if products have inadequate instructions, warnings, and labels. To overcome potential liability, companies provide customers fact sheets, manuals, warning labels, alerts, advice, guidance, counseling, and training. These interventions assist customers in the proper use, application, and installation of products and services.

COMPLYING WITH GOVERNMENT REGULATION

Government regulations and legislation force companies to provide, enhance, or limit customer education. The Surgeon General mandates warnings on every package of cigarettes. The Federal Aviation Administration (FAA) requires airlines to provide safety demonstrations and safety instruction cards for airline passengers. The Food and Drug Administration (FDA), the U.S. Department of Agriculture, and the Federal Trade Commission have laws governing product labeling. Other government organizations, such as the Consumer Product Safety Commission (CPSC) and the Occupational Safety and Health Administration (OSHA) decree information and warning labels for products, hazardous work sites, and equipment. State banking and insurance commissions regulate the language of loan agreements, insurance policies, and other financial contracts.

Failure to follow regulations can be costly. Agencies can levy fines, order changes in packaging and instruction manuals, or file lawsuits. Depending on your industry, you need to be familiar with the regulations listed in the *Code of Federal Regulations* (CFR). These codes, organized by federal agency, provide the guidelines for complying with federal regulations.

When it comes to customer education, the pharmaceutical industry is heavily regulated. The FDA reviews and approves all promotional and educational materials for medications. This includes the labeling on packages, patient package inserts (PPIs), brochures, advertisements, and other media. The FDA has three general rules that regulate the information pharmaceutical manufacturers communicate to their customers. First, the manufacturer must include a "brief summary" if the manufacturer names the drug and describes its use in communications materials. A brief summary is a long list of product data. The audience for brief summaries are both physicians and patients. However, the language of brief summaries is difficult for patients to read and comprehend. Second, the FDA does not require a brief summary if the communications educate customers about a disease without mentioning the drug by name or describing the drug's use. For example, Pfizer sponsored the publication of a book called *Help Yourself to Good Health.* The book does not mention Pfizer products, so there are no brief summaries in it. Third, the manufacturer must indicate the potential hazards of the product, as well as its limitations, if the manufacturer names a drug and describes its use.[14]

COMPLYING WITH INDUSTRY REGULATION

There are industry associations and regulatory bodies that regulate the form and purpose of customer education. The purpose of independent regulators is to ensure consumer protection and establish standards and practices. The Air Transportation Association, an industry association for aircraft builders and customers, formed a panel to determine how aircraft manufacturers develop maintenance training courses to teach customers how to repair and maintain aircraft. This panel produced guidelines for five levels of maintenance training, based on the depth of coverage needed:[15]

- General familiarization, covering maintenance procedures and methods for managers and non-maintenance personnel.
- Ramp and transit, covering maintenance methods for aircraft on the ground between flights.
- Line and base, covering overnight and extended aircraft maintenance.
- Specialized, covering special aircraft maintenance procedures.
- Overhaul, covering component-level maintenance procedures.

Commercial airline manufacturers, such as Boeing, typically focus on the first three levels, and the airlines themselves focus on the specialized courses. Specific system and component vendors provide training for the overhaul level. Other mandates by the ATA include using simple English as the language for all training materials and using specific "training blocks" within a course. A training block organizes content into the following related categories:

- Identification and location
- Purpose and interface
- Operation
- Functional description
- Maintenance practices
- Troubleshooting

The ATA enforces its mandates by specifying in airline contracts that all training to accompany the delivery of new aircraft be ATA-compliant.

Like the ATA, the New York Stock Exchange (NYSE) wields customer education rules over member organizations. Most of the NYSE's rules focus on protecting the investor. If a brokerage house, such as Merrill Lynch, wants to hold a customer seminar on an investing topic, it must follow several rules. Rule 405 states that only suitable investments can be recommended to customers. Paragraph 2478 requires a "Report of Speaking Activity" once the seminar concludes. The speaker must also adhere to standards of conduct, such as not recommending specific securities, keeping specific examples of investing separate from recommendations, and getting the topic approved by another NYSE member.[16]

Public Utility Commissions (PUC) maintain a love-hate relationship with the gas, electric, and water companies they regulate. On the love side of the fence, the PUC requires companies to provide customer education to enhance customer safety. This can include such things as how to light pilot lights, prevent electrocution, and avoid digging up pipes and wires. On the hate side of the fence, the PUC wants companies to provide conservation education, whereby an electric company teaches consumers to consume less of its product.

Operational Forces

Operational forces relate to customer interaction with the systems, structures, and attitudes that exist within your company. They can serve to teach your customers how to do business with you, reduce the cost of your services, and suppport your company's vision and values.

TEACHING CUSTOMERS HOW TO DO BUSINESS WITH YOU

If you talk with the people who deal with customers every day, you will uncover an interesting phenomenon: a lot of their time is spent teaching customers how to do business with the company. Think about it. In a big company, there could be 10-20 people a customer can contact just to conduct a normal business transaction. There are two sides to teaching customers how to do business with you: teaching customers how to accomplish the tasks they want to do, and teaching customers how you want them to do business with you.

Customer Tasks. Imagine the attitude of a customer who makes three separate phone calls to three different people in a company just to complete a task, such as scheduling a service call. This is a waste of time and will reduce customer satisfaction. If customers are having problems getting things done with your company, then you need to investigate whether education can help resolve the problem. Following are some common tasks customers want to accomplish:

- Obtaining product information
- Getting a product quote
- Finding where a product is sold
- Placing an order
- Resolving a mistake in an order
- Returning an order
- Scheduling a service call
- Getting help on how to use a product feature
- Resolving billing and invoice problems

Many companies publish booklets for customers that list the various tasks customers will want to accomplish, accompanied by the name and telephone number of the person who can best help them. Sales and customer service people can also help customers learn how to accomplish business tasks by knowing who can best handle the customer's request and why.

Company Systems. Companies have specific systems and processes for doing business. In many cases, it is the customer who must learn how the systems work, rather than the system bending to the specific needs of the customer. Here are some tasks for which customers must adapt to the company's way of doing things:

- Placing orders before deadlines
- Completing paperwork and forms correctly
- Possessing correct documents, such as a driver's license, to start new services
- Communicating product problems effectively
- Knowing legal, regulatory, and compliance procedures

It takes a picture ID to open a bank account, an old electric bill to get credit with the power company, and perfect impressions of car noises to get a car fixed correctly. Without this knowledge, customers will not be efficient in their dealings with companies. Companies are starting to recognize this problem. When you call a bank to open an account, the customer service person should remind you to bring a picture ID. The power company representative should explain its credit policies. But as for car noises, Ford Motor Company has a service brochure that helps you document your car's problems before you get to the shop. It even has boxes to check for noise categories so you do not have to mimic the sound yourself.

Remember that the more bureaucratic the organization is, the more effort it will take to teach the customer how to do business with it. For example, think of the government as a company and all of us citizens as customers. To apply for a passport, you have to know to bring pictures, your birth certificate, and a photo ID. To apply for a trademark, you need to know what class your trademark best fits, how to depict your trademark in graphic form, and how to research the existence of other similar trademarks. Filling out your taxes requires more knowledge and skills than most of us have. In all of these cases, knowledge of how the government does business drives customer success and efficiency.

REDUCING OR AVOIDING COSTS

Companies that do not teach customers how to use products successfully can incur significant costs. These costs come in the form of service calls, telephone support, product returns, and product liability lawsuits.

When Coleco introduced the Adam computer in the early 1980s, hundreds of customers who bought the computer returned it because they could not figure out how to use it. Coleco blamed the user manuals. By failing to make an investment in quality customer education, Coleco incurred the costs of handling product returns, increasing customer support, and redesigning user manuals. Coleco could have avoided these costs through better planning, design, and implementation of customer education.[17]

Another view of cost reduction is its effect on the cost of other customer services. A leading educational and entertainment software publisher estimates that if a customer calls its customer support line twice about how to use a product, the calls eliminate the profit on that product. The math is shown in Exhibit 4–2. The retail price of an educational or entertainment software program is $50. Wholesale price is about half of that, or $25. Cost of goods sold, including such things as sales costs, packaging, disk duplication, and author royalties, is half the wholesale cost, or $12.50. The remaining $12.50 is contribution toward fixed expenses. If each support call's average cost is $7, then two calls cost $14, or $1.50 more than the contribution. By improving customer education methods and identifying opportunities where customer education can ease the burden on other systems, you can reduce costs and possibly redeploy staff.

PROMOTING THE COMPANY'S VISION AND VALUES

Companies want their customers to have a certain impression about them: easiest to do business with, safest products, law abiding, or every-

Exhibit 4–2   Effects of Support Calls on Product Profits

Retail price	$50.00
Wholesale price	25.00
Revenues	$25.00
Cost of goods sold	12.50
Contribution margin	$12.50
Supports calls (2 @ $7)	14.00
Effect on profits	– $1.50

day low prices. Perceptions customers form about a company come from their experiences with that company, the messages the company communicates, and the actions of the company. The images customers perceive should link directly to the vision and values of the company leaders.

If a company claims to have the utmost concern for customer safety, you expect that company to do things that reinforce that claim. The company might spend millions of dollars engineering a product to reduce the risk of accidental injury, similar to what Genie did with its garage-door opener. But, as Genie discovered, there is only so much engineering you can do to make it a safe product. A chain saw is inherently dangerous and no amount of engineering will make it completely safe. Customer education can lead to safer use of the product and enhance the company's safety image.

Stihl Chainsaw did just that. Stihl views itself as the marketer of the world's safest chainsaws. Stihl's products have the typical instruction manuals and safety guides but its distribution methods set it apart. When you buy a Stihl saw from a distributor, you cannot grab a box and pay for it at the cashier. Rather, before you get out the door, a salesperson demonstrates how to remove and install the chain, clean the saw, ensure that the saw is oiling the chain correctly, start the saw, stop the saw, and engage and disengage safety devices. Woodcutting safety tips are also thrown in. Stihl requires the salesperson to do this training. This process instills Stihl's commitment that its customers will have a lower incidence of chain saw accidents than its competitors. It also reinforces its image as the safest chain saw on the market.

R.J. Reynolds Tobacco Company (RJR) has used customer education as a means to reinforce its image as a law-abiding company. In the wake of consumer concerns over underage smoking and threatened government regulation to place tobacco under the jurisdiction of the Food and Drug Administration (FDA), RJR introduced a 12-page brochure and a youth education kit designed to teach children how to resist peer pressure to smoke. The education kit also reinforces existing laws in 50 states that deny children access to tobacco products. RJR's agenda is to keep tobacco regulation out of the FDA's hands. But to do that, RJR has to convince citizens that it is law abiding and that it is doing something to ensure that children and adults comply with the law. The brochure and youth education kit, as well as the advertising campaign, are the means for RJR to achieve its aims.[18]

Restraining Forces

A discussion of driving forces is incomplete without presenting the typical restraining forces that prevent customer education from happening. The three primary restraining forces mentioned here are investment, lack of know-how, and product familiarity.

NO RETURN ON INVESTMENT

The first question any idea, plan, or proposal will raise is, "How much will it cost?" Of all the restraining forces, cost is the one that holds back the driving forces most often. Decision makers need to know how customer education will return the investment. Will it generate greater revenue? Sell more product? Show gains in market share? Reduce costs? Reduce liability? Whereas many investments have an immediate effect on the bottom line, organizations might realize some returns, such as reduced liability, only years in the future.

Overcoming cost restraints requires that your customer education plan plainly state the return on investment. Of course, investments always have risks and are never guaranteed. The defense of your plan requires careful analysis and conservative estimation. You can establish a budget for customer education by performing a financial analysis. Determine the availability of capital and balance the costs with the possible returns. Consider creating two analyses, a base case and a conservative case.

Only invest what is really needed to resolve the need you identified. A one-page instruction sheet is significantly less expensive than a 30-minute video, yet each addresses different learning needs. You must balance the investment with the outcomes you want to achieve.

INEXPERIENCE WITH CUSTOMER EDUCATION

The lack of know-how means the knowledge and skills to create quality customer education does not exist within the organization. It can range from the ability to conduct analyses of learner needs, selection of instructional theories and strategies, development of the materials, implementation of the program, and evaluation to measure effectiveness. If the company lacks experience in designing and implementing customer education do not let it stop you if you believe customer education is the right thing to do. Instructional design consultants can help you get a program started, and this book can ensure that you are heading in the right direction.

CUSTOMERS KNOW OUR PRODUCT ALREADY— WHAT MORE CAN WE TEACH THEM?

Customers' familiarity with a product or product class can restrain the development of customer education. If customers are familiar with a product, we assume that they have the knowledge and skills to function competently. However, the effect of familiarity can be misjudged. Consider what happens when you rent a car. It takes a while to function competently in the rental car. You struggle to figure out how to turn on the headlights, operate the cruise control, tune the radio, or even remove the keys from the ignition. Even though most adults are familiar with the task of driving and with the general operations of cars, they are unfamiliar with the environment of the rental car. Thus, there is a potential need for customer education.

Balancing Driving and Restraining Forces

With driving forces pushing you to adopt customer education and restraining forces holding you back, what do you do to make a decision? Recognizing that there are driving and restraining forces is the first step, but now the trick is to weight the relative value of them both. The side with the most points wins.

A helpful tool to perform this analysis is the driving force/restraining force diagram shown in Exhibit 4–3. On the left side of the chart, draw bars representing the driving forces. You determine the length of the bar by a relative value you assign to the force, usually on a scale of ten. A value of ten means that the importance of the force is very high, whereas a value of one means the importance is low. Assign these yourself, or do a survey of your co-workers or your customers to get their input.

On the right side of the chart, draw bars representing the restraining forces. Each driving force does not need a corresponding restraining force. The balance between driving and restraining is an aggregate of all the forces on both sides. In this case, driving forces have an aggregate value of 13, and restraining forces have an aggregate of 10.

Exhibit 4–3   Driving and Restraining Forces Analysis

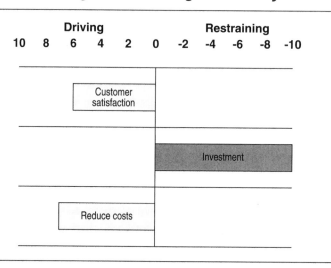

Exhibit 4–4   Alternative Driving and Restraining Forces Analysis

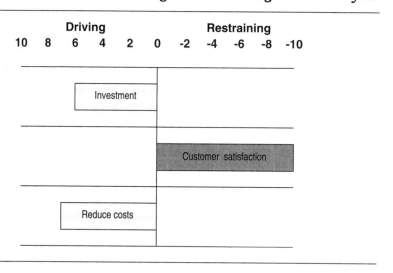

This rough analysis shows the forces definitely favor a customer education solution.

As you think through the driving and restraining forces surrounding a problem, play with their relationship in order to simulate other effects, as shown in Exhibit 4–4. For instance, you might analyze a problem and discover that the company wants to reduce costs and that the money to do so is available. In this case, investment is a driving force. However, the training course you plan, although cheaper, might not provide the same level of support as ten customer service people. If this happens, customer satisfaction could drop, whereby satisfaction becomes a restraining force in your equation. As illustrated in this example, typical driving forces can become restraining forces, depending on the problem and the context. The driving and restraining forces discussed in this chapter are the raw materials for you to begin analyzing the worth of customer education in your own company.

Summary

The key concepts to take away from this chapter are as follows:

- Three kinds of forces drive the need for customer education: marketing forces, legal forces, and organizational forces.
- Marketing forces relate to improving customer satisfaction, stimulating the demand for products, differentiating products from the competition, and correcting consumer misconceptions.
- Legal forces relate to product liability, government regulation, and industry regulation.
- Operational forces relate to teaching customers how to do business with you, reducing or avoiding costs, and promoting the company's vision and values.
- Balancing the driving forces are restraining forces. These include lack of a return on investment, not knowing how to develop customer education, and assuming that customers are already educated.

The Process of Customer Education

There is a German folk legend of a device called the Nurnberg Funnel that allows you to pour knowledge and skills right into someone's head. You attach the funnel, select your favorite knowledge, and pour it in: nuclear physics, biochemistry, modern dance, or the perfect golf stroke. We all recognize that such a device is fantasy, but according to John Carroll, author of *The Nurnberg Funnel,* companies often develop customer education solutions that mimic the funnel by trying to pour knowledge rapidly into customers' heads. Yet, as Carroll points out, "given what we understand about human intelligence and learning, the very idea of 'pouring' material into the mind seems ill-conceived."[1]

Overloading the customer with comprehensive knowledge and skills for a product in one sitting is counterproductive. Rather, you must divide and conquer—providing the customer with the appropriate knowledge and skills at the time they need them. This chapter examines a model for designing customer education strategies, drawing heavily on consumer behavior research. It traces how customer education flows through the natural relationship you establish with customers, starting at goal formation, continuing through acquisition and consumption, and ending at disposition.

The Comprehensive Theory of Choice

Think, for a moment, about your experiences as a consumer. First, you feel a need. For instance, you are hungry. Next, you think of all those things that will satisfy your hunger: Moonpies, a homemade turkey dinner, pizza and beer at the corner pizzeria, Lean Cuisine, and so on. At this time (coincidentally) a TV commercial touts the health benefits of Lean Cuisine. You are feeling out of shape and you are too tired to cook, so you make your selection, the Lean Cuisine. You run off to the store, buy the product, and return home. After a quick read of the instructions, you nuke the package in the microwave for a couple of minutes, then sit down to eat. Once finished, cleanup is easy; you toss what remains into the trash.

As illustrated by this example, consumption is a series of sequential phases that take the consumer from a need all the way to disposing of what remains of a product. In consumer behavior circles, these phases— goal formation, acquisition, consumption, and disposition—are referred to as the *comprehensive theory of choice.*[2] (See Exhibit 5-1.)

Here is how these phases map to the situation described above. Goal formation was the phase when you first exhibited a need, narrowed down the possible options that could resolve the need, then decided that Lean Cuisine was the option for you. Once those tasks were complete, you moved to the acquisition phase. Here, you had to determine where to get the product, how to pay for it, and how to get it home. Once you got the product home, you moved to the consumption phase, where you prepared the product and ate it. Finally, when you were finished eating and ready to clean up the mess, you moved into the disposition phase.

An opportunity for customer education exists at each one of these phases. Teaching customers about the nutritional content of a product influences goal formation. Giving clear directions on how to get to your

Exhibit 5-1   The Comprehensive Theory of Choice

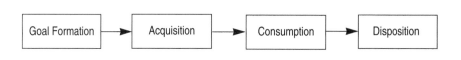

store facilitates acquisition. Instructions for preparing the product serves consumption. And instructions for proper disposal affects disposition. For the designer of customer education strategies, these phases provide a simple, yet comprehensive, guide to help plan complete customer education systems that exist throughout the relationship with the customer.

GOAL FORMATION

Remember when you were a child, standing in front of the candy counter trying to decide which candy to buy? Would it be a candy bar, a pack of gum, or a jaw breaker? Goal formation includes all of those soul-searching activities in which customers engage *before* acquiring a product. During goal formation, customers seek to answer questions such as, What do I need? Do I need it now? What will resolve the need? Which one will work best for me?

There are four phases to goal formation: desire, priority, preference, and intention (See Exhibit 5–2.) Desire is the formation of needs. Priority is the importance of a need. Preference is the selection of products that can resolve the need. Intention is the plan to buy. This section shows how customer education plays a role in helping resolve the customer's need for knowledge and skills at each of these phases.

Desire. Desire formation is tightly linked to customer needs. That is, customers desire something to fill a gap in their life. During the desire phase, customer education can help customers recognize needs. When customers recognize they have a need, they have learned an attitude. For example, to sell perfume, Chanel uses advertising to teach

Exhibit 5–2   Components of Goal Formation

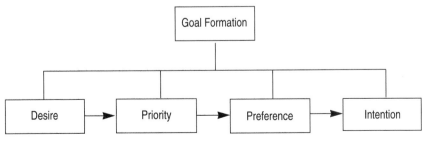

customers the need for love and belongingness. To sell customized business papers, Paper Direct uses its catalog to teach customers the need for self-esteem.

Priority. Once customers learn they have a need, they will determine the importance, or priority, of resolving the need. Establishing priority is typically internal to the customer's own decision-making process. However, customer education can help push the customer to give a need a higher priority.

One form of priority education is letting customers know a solution exists to resolve their need. Imagine that it takes you several hours to prepare dinner for your family every evening, because you have to chop all the food by hand with a knife. You need to reduce the time it takes to prepare dinner so you can spend more time with your family. The need, however, has a low priority, because you are not aware of any other way to chop food. Then one day you learn about food processors from an article in the local paper. Suddenly the priority of the need for a food processor is very high. Customer education through the newspaper article contributed to strengthening the priority.

The second form of priority education, called *situational education,* is keeping customers abreast of trends in order to help them prioritize their needs. For example, investment advisors pass along articles about the rising cost of education and project on their portable computers the future cost of a college education to shape prioritization of parents' investment needs. It is eye-opening to learn that to afford a college education 15-18 years from now, you must invest several hundred dollars each month. Investment firms teach parents this because it increases the likelihood that they will invest rather than buy a new sports car. Customer education is one means of helping customers prioritize needs in line with your own sales aims.

Preference. Once a need has high priority, the customer needs help in figuring out which product best resolves the need. This is preference formation, where the customer searches for information about the best products.

Preference formation is usually the strongest focus for customer education in the goal formation phase. Customers are looking for reasons to buy (or not buy) your product. They want to know how your product works, its features and benefits, and its advantages and disadvantages compared to the competition. Salespeople, advertisements, and product literature—promotional components of customer education—are the customer's sources for this type of learning.

Intentions. Through preference formation, the customer selected a product and is ready to buy. However, the customer's ability to afford the product and the time frame in which he or she needs the product affects the culminating intention to buy. For instance, you walk into a corner store after a heavy garlic pasta lunch to buy some breath mints. You make your selection, then go to the clerk and find you have no cash to pay for them. You then sheepishly return the product to the box and leave the store. You intended to buy but lacked money to complete the transaction. The same holds true for time. Perhaps you have enough money for the mints, but while you wait in line, your bus pulls up outside. Catching the bus is more important then the mints, so you leave without completing the transaction.

Customer education plays an important role during intention formation. It acts as a cost control by preventing unqualified customers from getting to the acquisition phase. Once in the acquisition phase, the costs to acquire the order kick in. If the customer cannot complete the acquisition, then you cannot recoup those costs. For example, five days before Christmas you spot the perfect gift for Aunt Martha in a catalog. The price is right, so you call to place you order. Unfortunately, you learn that the product will take 10 working days to reach Aunt Martha. You thank the clerk and hang up the phone, abandoning your intention to buy. For the catalog firm, the costs associated with that phone call—operator time and long-distance charges—are unrecoverable because the customer did not buy. To limit such costs, it is imperative to educate customers about details of price and shipping time before they get to the acquisition phase.

GOAL FORMATION SOLUTION

The Charles Schwab & Co. Mutual Fund Selection Guide™ exemplifies how customer education can address each phase of goal formation to help customers identify needs, set priorities, narrow down preferences, and plan intentions. (See Exhibit 5–3.)

Identifying Needs. There are two tools to help the customer answer the question, "Do I need an investment plan?" First, a questionnaire asks the customer about his or her income, age, and propensity for risk. The

Exhibit 5-3   Charles Schwab & Co. Mutual Fund Selection Guide™

1 Complete this questionnaire.

2 Select your investment plan.

3 Choose your funds.

4 Put your plan into action.

How to choose SchwabFunds.

As you'll see from the chart on Step 3 of 4 ("Choose Your Funds"), Schwab's own fund family includes funds which match each of the categories in your investment plan. You may want to use SchwabFunds exclusively, or use them in combination with *Select List* funds.

You'll find more information about SchwabFunds on the back of this Planner.

How to choose *Select List* funds.

The *Select List* column in Step 3 of this *Planner* ("Choose Your Funds"), is designed to help you find funds on Schwab's Mutual Fund *Select List*.

The Select List is published quarterly on:

February 15	*August 15*
May 15	*November 15*

If a Select List does not accompany this Planner or is out of date, you can request the most current issue at your nearest Schwab office or call

1-800-2 NO-LOAD.

To choose funds from the *Select List*, just open it up and look for the fund categories shown on the chart.

For example, mutual funds shown on the *Select List* under "Small Company" and "Aggressive Growth" categories generally contain a large percentage of small company stocks. So, to fill the small company stock portion of your investment plan, you may want to consider the funds in these categories.

Keep in mind, of course, that the types of stocks or bonds held by individual funds within the same fund category may vary widely. A prospectus for each fund will give you more complete information about the types of stocks and bonds contained in each fund. You can obtain a free prospectus by calling Schwab at

1-800-2 NO-LOAD.

Please read the prospectus carefully before you invest.

second tool is a table balancing the customer's score on the question-naire against five investment scenarios. For example, a score of 25 calls for a conservative plan; a score of 92 calls for an aggressive plan. For each of these plans, there is a profile of the type of investor best suited for the plan, principles for diversification of investments, and projections of returns on the investment. Recognizing a need is attitudinal learning. Schwab's solution provides the knowledge and skills to help a customer decide whether he or she needs an investment plan.

Setting Priority. Convincing the customer that an investment plan is a high priority is very subtle in Schwab's guide. One method is mentioning the 20-year average return on investment for each plan. It connotes a sense of urgency for the customer to get on board early. Another method is the structure of the guide, which portrays investment plan-ning as a simple, four-step process. Urgency and ease of use are two factors that help propel needs to the top of the customer's priority list.

Narrowing Down Preferences. Once the need for an investment plan is a priority, Schwab's task is to guide the customer to the products that meet investment plan objectives and help the customer decide how to allocate assets. To achieve the first aim, Schwab presents a table of the different mutual fund investment options available to the investor: large company stocks, small company stocks, international stocks, bonds, and cash. Here the customer learns about the available products, and Schwab promotes its own mutual fund products. Schwab is careful to direct the customer to acquire a fund prospectus before selecting an investment vehicle. To achieve the second aim, allocation of assets, Schwab pro-vides a worksheet that helps the customer allocate assets in the proper percentages and encourages the customer to list the investments to pur-chase. Clear instructions help customers complete this worksheet.

Planning Intentions. The only limiting factor that will prevent a customer from completing a transaction with Schwab is the $1,000 minimum pur-chase requirement per fund. Schwab teaches customers about this in the worksheet instructions.

ACQUISITION

In the acquisition phase, the customer has decided to buy your product. However, there are three issues you must help the customer resolve:

1. How to access the product.

2. How to buy the product.

3. How to get the product home (or to a place of business).

Access. Access is getting to where you can purchase the product. This might involve driving to a store, arranging a visit from a sales rep, securing a catalog, or calling an 800-number. Customer education can facilitate access to products. For example, advertisements or sales sheets can list retail stores carrying the product, and 800-number telephone services can direct customers to sources. Perhaps the most valuable form of customer education for facilitating access is a good set of directions: from a clerk over the phone, on a brochure (with a map), or a person in the store to show the exact shelf location of a product.

Exchange. Once a customer has located the product, he or she must make an exchange to own the product. Typically, the exchange involves money or the promise to pay for the goods or services one desires. To facilitate an exchange, customers need to know how to do business with your company. For example, if your company requires certain information from customers to process a transaction, customers need to know it ahead of time, or they will get frustrated when they try to consumate the deal. In addition, a lack of information could cause errors with their order. Therefore, providing customers tools to facilitate the interaction, such as an order form, or meeting customers to explain your processes and needs, are learning opportunities that can overcome problems in your everyday dealings with customers. Additionally, your customer service and sales people need to be trained to recognize opportunities

Exhibit 5–4   Components of Acquisition

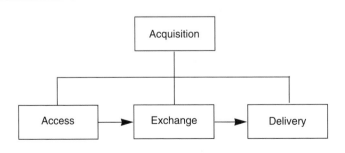

for teaching customers about your business and making that knowledge stick.

If you use a contract to govern an exchange, keep in mind that contracts can be difficult for customers to understand. Many customers do not know legal terminology, and the long sentence structure of legal writing is difficult to interpret. To make contracts clearer and to maintain the legal integrity of the contract, a method of contractual writing called "plain language" or "plain English" has been legislated in many states.[3] The aim of plain language is, "to put consumers on a more equal footing with industry when they sign personal business contracts."[4] Through the use of simple sentences, common terminology, and visual elements such as headlines, subheads, numbering, graphs, and separation lines, contracts are easier for consumers to read and for salespeople to teach.

Delivery. Delivery is when a customer takes possession of goods. Delivery is usually simple, but for industrial goods and international deliveries, customer education can help overcome some common problems. For example, what if you took delivery of goods that required frozen storage at –50°F, and your freezer went down to only –20°F? What if you received a sofa that was 60 inches wide, and your doors were only 48 inches wide? Or if you received a 5,000 pound pallet, and your forklift handled only 2,000 pounds? Sellers should make it plain to buyers the requirements or options for accepting delivery of goods. This can occur through product literature or salesperson communications with the customer. For international transactions, delivery is a confusing process involving national and international laws, tariffs, duties, taxes, and cultural norms. For the United States alone, there are more than 500 pages of customs regulations governing the delivery of international goods. A seller with experience trading in certain countries might offer seminars to customers to help them better understand import and export requirements.

CONSUMPTION

The customer now owns the product, and all that stands in the way of resolving the original need is the knowledge and skill to put the product to use. During the consumption phase, customers need to know how to prepare the product, how to use the product, how to maintain the

Exhibit 5–5   Components of Consumption

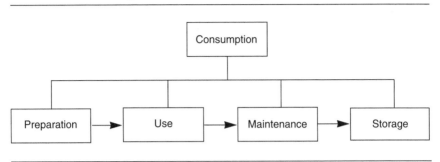

product, and how to store the product. (See Exhibit 5–5.) During this phase, *product training* is perhaps the term that best describes the role of customer education.

Preparation. During the preparation phase, the customer prepares the product for use. This might include assembling the product, installing the product, or transforming the product.

- **Assembly tasks** involve putting together the pieces of the product. For a computer, the customer has to plug in various components and copy the necessary operating and application software.
- **Installation tasks** involve installing a pre-assembled product. For a car battery, the customer has to put the battery into the car, screw down the battery retainer, and connect the appropriate wires.
- **Transformation tasks** involve changing a product from one form to another. For a frozen dinner, the customer has to transform the product from being frozen to being heated.

The aim of customer education during the preparation phase is to help customers learn the nomenclature of the product and the procedure for assembly, installation, or transformation. Nomenclature names the various parts of the product and is typically taught through pictures and diagrams. A procedure is a sequence of two to nine specific instructions with a certain result—a correctly assembled, installed, or transformed product. For instance, the procedure for installing a car battery might read as follows:

1. Place battery into the battery holder. Make sure the positive terminal is to the left, and the negative terminal is to the right.

2. Tighten the battery retainer to secure the battery into place.
3. Put the negative connector cable on the negative terminal and tighten.
4. Put the positive connector cable on the positive terminal and tighten.

Use. Once the customer correctly prepares a product, it is ready for use. This is the phase in which the customer uses a product to resolve the need identified during goal formation. The aim of customer education, then, is to enable the customer to effectively use a product. The risk of not effectively teaching the customer how to use a product is substantial, as Coleco found with its Adam® computer. Customers found the Adam's instruction manuals so poor that they could not use their new computers to resolve their needs. Ultimately, customers returned the product in droves. For the use phase, you should consider customer education strategies that address two kinds of learning: functional and artistic.

Functional learning focuses on enabling the customer to achieve specific results with a product, and **artistic learning** focuses on stimulating ideas for using a product in new and creative ways. Through functional learning the customer learns the basics of product operation (e.g., programming a VCR, setting the time on a digital clock, or printing a file from your personal computer). Instruction manuals and introductory classes typically address functional learning topics. Artistic learning, on the other hand, teaches customers to be innovative with a product. For instance, software companies sponsor workshops to teach customers how to apply software in unique ways. Similarly, Home Depot holds weekly seminars to teach customers about do-it-yourself projects. Seminars, user bulletins, newsletters, and other methods typically provide the content for artistic learning.

State-of-the-art scientific instruments typify the functional-artistic relationship. For an instrument such as a thermal cycler (a device for amplifying DNA), there is a level of functional knowledge a customer must have in order to use the instrument correctly. Loading samples, setting up methods, and analyzing data are all functional skills. However, providing customers insight into the science of DNA amplification, such as chemical mixtures, thermal protocols, and detection strategies, takes them beyond button pushing to creative problem solving. Keep in mind that if a technology is new, the company that invented it is the de facto expert on its use. The company's role, then, is to transfer its know-how to the customer to enable the customer to achieve breakthrough results.

Maintenance. For long life and years of trouble-free use, many products require maintenance. Maintenance can be as simple as changing the oil in your car every 3,000 miles, or as complex as overhauling an aircraft engine. It even includes fixing products when they break. We can classify maintenance into two categories, prevention and repair.

The aim of customer education for prevention is to assure continuous, satisfactory performance of a product. It involves teaching the customer a maintenance schedule, plus the skills for conducting the maintenance. For instance, the instruction manual for a car details the exact maintenance a car needs every x number of miles and shows the customer how to perform the simpler maintenance tasks. On a different scale, Boeing's maintenance education for new aircraft is six weeks in duration.

The aim of customer education for repair is to get broken products running again. It involves teaching customers how to troubleshoot, disassemble, and reassemble a product. Some companies prefer not to teach customers these skills, due to the complexity of the product or to assure work for their service departments. However, other companies, such as International Game Technology (IGT), a gaming equipment manufacturer, have an extensive curriculum to teach customers how to repair their machines. IGT's courses range from on-the-floor repair of coin jams to troubleshooting malfunctioning electronics.

For both prevention and repair, a key channel for educating customers is service technicians. Service technicians visit customers to repair equipment, so they are in a position to communicate knowledge to customers. For instance, a service technician for photocopiers can teach customers how to clean the glass, install new toner cartridges, and perform simple repairs, such as extracting jammed paper.

Storage. Before preparation and after use, customers need to know how to store a product. This is especially important with food items, dangerous products, such as chemicals and medicines, and mechanical devices that sit idle for long periods. The aim of customer education for storage is to ensure a product remains ready for use for a given time. The simple instruction, "Refrigerate after opening," clearly tells customers how to store a product. For mechanical products such as snow blowers and lawn mowers, the seasons dictate that the customer will store the product for a certain period. During the off season, proper storage might include cleaning components, draining oil, and sealing intakes. Remember, however, that if you teach customers how to store a product, you must also teach them how to re-prepare the product after storage. For food products, this might involve reheating the product. For mechanical products, customers might have to add lubrication fluids or verify the integrity of parts.

DISPOSITION

Disposition is the final phase in the consumption process-customers trashing, recycling, selling, or giving away the product. (See Exhibit 5-6.) In the age of environmental awareness, teaching customers how to get rid of products has renewed importance. Customers should know what the disposal options are for a product and the strengths and weaknesses of those options. They should also know the laws regulating disposal of certain products, especially for hazardous materials.

Trash. For a product that no one will ever use again, one can put the product in the trash to have it hauled away or personally take it to the local landfill. The aim for customer education focuses on making sure people trash a product the right way. Instructions can be simple, such as messages on product wrappers that read, "Dispose of Properly" or "Put litter in its place." Or they can be quite complex, illustrated by disposal instructions found on material safety data sheets that accompany hazardous chemicals. Legislation from federal and state agencies govern

Exhibit 5-6   Components of Disposition

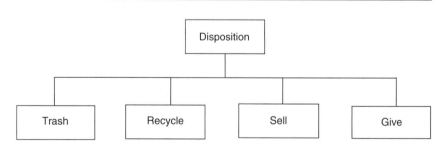

many disposal practices. To help customers navigate these laws, Safety-Kleen runs an extensive seminar program to teach customers how to comply with disposal regulations.

Recycle. Recycling involves transforming a used product into something else. Empty aluminum cans might be transformed into new cans, used plastic bottles might be transformed into fence posts or lawn furniture, and old tires might be cut up and used as cushioning under playground equipment. An aim of customer education for recycling is motivating people to recycle. Another is to teach customers that a product is recyclable, most often by using the recycling symbol. To change customer attitudes about recycling, some companies have invented elaborate programs, such as the Aluminum Company of America (ALCOA) exhibit, called the A-Maze-Ing Aluminum Can Recycling Factory, which taught the process and purpose of recycling. In the exhibit, a person first learns the skill of testing cans with a refrigerator magnet to see if they are aluminum or bi-metal. Next, the person takes the role of an empty aluminum can and crawls through the factory, experiencing the can crusher, the slicer, and the melter. Then, wrapped in a costume resembling a new can, the person emerges from the factory to be filled up with their favorite beverage.[5]

Sell. Selling involves transferring ownership of a product through an exchange. The resellers who carry your products do this every day. Individuals sell their used cars or trade them in on a newer model. The aim of customer education for selling is to teach customers how to sell your products. Hart Schaffner & Marx (HSM) has its own university to teach its customers—retail clothiers and tailors—how to sell men's suits.[6] The program gives HSM more control at the point of sale over the end customer, strengthens its partnership with retailers, and highlights the quality of its suits. The curriculum covers general business topics such as business planning and store management, product features and how best to fit customers, and sales and service skills.

Give. Giving involves transferring ownership of a product without an exchange. An example of this is giving used products to charitable organizations such as church groups, Goodwill, or the Salvation Army. As with selling, the aim of customer education for giving is making customers aware of how they can donate items to these organizations.

Applying the Theory to Design Customer Education Strategies

The comprehensive theory of choice is your map for designing customer education strategies. Successful customer education requires achievable performance objectives and a meaningful, systematic, and process-oriented plan. By determining what a customer needs to know during goal formation, acquisition, consumption, and disposition, your strategy will be comprehensive and complete.

PERFORMANCE OBJECTIVES

A performance objective clearly describes the behaviors you want customers to demonstrate after they receive instruction.[7] Objectives stem from the needs identified in the gap analysis. The purpose of objectives is to point toward an instructional solution that enables customers to achieve the goal. Flawed objectives usually lead to flawed instruction.

For example, a needs analysis reveals that customers cannot correctly assemble a backyard swing set. The cause of the problem is that customers do not know the procedure for assembling the swing set. An objective for this need is, "Customers will assemble a backyard swing set." While this objective succinctly states what the customer's behavior will be after instruction, it is fuzzy. There is no mention of how long it should take a customer to assemble the product. Nor is there any mention of the conditions required for success or how long the behavior will take.

A model for writing clear, meaningful objectives is the ABCD model:[8]

- Audience: Who will perform the behavior.
- Behavior: The specific task you want the audience to perform.
- Conditions: What resources the customer will have to help perform the behavior, or the situation in which the customer will perform the behavior.
- Degree: The measure of how well or how quickly the customer must perform the behavior.

Exhibit 5–7 illustrates some common elements and an example for each of these components.

You can see the difference between the original "fuzzy" objective and the revised statement using the ABCD model. For the audience components, knowing who will perform the behavior ensures your

Exhibit 5–7   The ABCD Method for Writing Goal Statements

Component	Common Elements	Example
Audience	• Age • Experience • Skills and knowledge • Physical handicaps • Geographics	Customers in the United States over the age of 18 with an eighth-grade reading level.
Behavior	• Knowledge • Skills • Attitudes	Assemble a backyard swing set.
Conditions	• Location • Resources • Tools	Outside on their lawn, using a phillips-head screwdriver, with no helper.
Degree	• Quality • Quantity • Time • Money	Assembly complete in less than one hour and performed so the swing set will not collapse.

instruction meets their needs. For instance, your instruction would be useless if your audience were Spanish-speaking, but your instruction was written for English speakers. The same is true for conditions. If the instruction implies that a single person could perform the task, but in reality it takes three people to complete it, then your customer will not be able to perform the task. The other benefit of the ABCD objective is that it specifies a measure for acceptable performance. This will ultimately tell you if your strategy worked.

Whether your objectives are fuzzy or detailed depends on how the objectives will ultimately be used. In some cases, the purpose of objectives is to serve as signposts, or placeholders. These objectives are typically fuzzy, because specific details are not necessary. In other cases, objectives serve as the blueprint for designing a learning system. These objectives must be specific to ensure the development of quality learning events.

Remember that objectives focus on results, not activities. Write them to describe what customers will do, not how they will do it. For instance, the statement, "Customers will take a three-day course to learn to assemble products" is not an objective, because it focuses on how customers will learn.

THE STRATEGY DESIGN MATRIX

The core organizing structure for customer education strategy planning is the strategy design matrix. The matrix is a table listing the components of goal formation, acquisition, consumption, and disposition down the vertical axis, and the three types of customers across the horizontal axis. The purpose of the design matrix is to organize what customers need to learn, when they need to learn, and who needs to learn. The matrix for each phase is shown in Exhibit 5–8. The variables of when to educate and whom to educate are the columns and rows in the matrix. What you teach—the objectives—is entered in the empty cells.

Exhibit 5–8   Strategy Design Matrix

	Buyer	User	Reseller
Goal Formation			
Desire			
Priority			
Preference			
Intention			
Acquisition			
Access			
Exchange			
Delivery			
Consumption			
Preparation			
Use			
Maintenance			
Storage			
Disposition			
Trash			
Recycle			
Sell			
Give			

CASE IN STRATEGY DESIGN: AUNTIEA'S BED&BODY® WARMER

AuntieA's is a small, family-owned manufacturer in Reno, Nevada. Its primary product is the Bed&Body Warmer, a cotton bag 24" long by 7" wide that is filled with natural grains and spices. You heat the Bed&Body Warmer in a microwave oven for three to four minutes. It then stays warm—above 115°F—for an hour or more. People use the Bed&Body Warmer to warm their bed, warm their feet, and ease their tense and sore muscles. AuntieA's primarily sells its products through catalogs and retailers. However, it does sell a few products directly to end users. Here's how AuntieA's performed a strategy design for the Bed&Body Warmer. Note that the objectives here are primarily sign-posts, and thus are less detailed than ABCD objectives.

Exhibit 5–9 lists the primary objectives for the goal formation phases. For desire formation, the objectives focus on getting the customer to realize physiological needs related to warmth and health care. Notice that the audience specified in each objective is different for each customer. The objectives for priority formation are the same for each customer, concentrating on making customers aware that a specific product class exists to address the need. Preference objectives for each customer relate primarily to learning facts about the product that will help the customer favorably compare the Bed&Body Warmer to competitive products. The additional preference objectives for resellers show how they will make a profit by carrying the product. The objectives for intentions relate to the seasonality of the product. Many customers refuse to buy during the warmer months because the product does not seem necessary in the summer. Who wants a bed warmer when it is 90°F outside? Making customers aware that the Bed&Body Warmer also relieves physical ailments year round is one strategy to overcome time-based purchase intentions.

Exhibit 5–10 lists the primary objectives for the acquisition phase. For access, each of the customer types need to know where they can get the product and how they go about placing an order. AuntieA's has relatively little contact with the buyer and user, so there is not much to teach those customers during the exchange and delivery phases. However, resellers must know pricing levels and credit terms in order to facilitate an exchange, as well as shipping methods, packaging, and delivery time to facilitate delivery. Exhibit 5–11 lists the objectives for the consumption phases. Buyers and resellers typically do not consume the product as end users, so all of the objectives relating to preparation,

Exhibit 5–9   Goal Formation Matrix for the Bed&Body Warmer

	Buyer	User	Reseller
Desire	• Realizes a friend's or loved one's need for warmth and comfort. • Realizes a friend's or loved one's need to ease the pain of various physical ailments.	• Realizes personal need for warmth and comfort. • Realizes personal need to ease the pain of various physical ailments.	• Realizes the market's need for warmth and comfort. • Realizes the market's need to ease the pain of various physical ailments.
Priority	• Awareness that a product class for microwave heating bags exists.	• Awareness that a product class for microwave heating bags exists.	• Awareness that a product class for microwave heating bags exists.
Preference	• States facts about the product. • States features of the product. • States benefits of the product. • States the price of the product.	• States facts about the product. • States features of the product. • States benefits of the product. • States the price of the product.	• States facts about the product. • States features of the product. • States benefits of the product. • States the price of the product and volume discount levels. • Calculates margin for the product • States the terms of sale. • States the available quantities.
Intention	• States alternative product uses during warm seasons.	• States alternative product uses during warm seasons.	• States alternative product uses during warm seasons.

Exhibit 5–10   Acquisition Matrix for the Bed&Body Warmer

	Buyer	User	Reseller
Access	• Names one retail outlet carrying the product. • Locates the retail outlet carrying the product.	• Names one retail outlet carrying the product. • Locates the retail outlet carrying the product.	• Uses the correct phone or fax number or e-mail address to place an order directly with the company. • States the name and phone number of their sales representative.
Exchange	NA	NA	• States the whole-sale price and volume discount levels. • Describes payment terms. • Describes how and when it can contact the company to place order.
Delivery	NA	NA	• Selects a best-way shipper. • States the size and weight of what will be delivered. • States the delivery date.

use, and maintenance are directed toward the user. For preparation, users must determine whether they can use the product based on the health risks of heat therapy. They must also know how to warm the product. During use, users must know how to use the product safely. Maintenance of the product is very simple, with the flannel cover being the only part of the product that requires maintenance. Storage, however, relates to each of the customers. Buyers and resellers must know

Exhibit 5–11   Consumption Matrix for the Bed&Body Warmer

	Buyer	User	Reseller
Preparation	NA	• Evaluates the health precautions. • Warms the product safely.	NA
Use	NA	• Applies the product to the body without causing injury.	NA
Maintenance	NA	• Washes the flannel cover so it will not shrink or fade.	NA
Storage	• Stores the product in a cool, dry place.	• Stores the product in a cool, dry place.	• Stores the product in a cool, dry place.

how to store the product before giving or selling it, and users must know how to store the product while it is not in use.

Exhibit 5–12 lists the objectives for the disposition components. The only customer who will ultimately trash the product is the user. For this, the user needs to know that the product does not require any special means of disposal. Ideally, customers could toss it in a compost heap. There are no recyclable components of the product, thus there are no objectives for this component. Selling relates entirely to the reseller, so here the objectives focus on how AuntieA's can help resellers better sell the product. Giving relates entirely to the buyer, so teaching buyers to whom they can give a Bed&Body Warmer is an objective for this component.

The objectives specified in these four matrices were the starting point for AuntieA's customer education strategy. Further refinement of the objectives using the ABCD methodology made them more specific and established measures that provided benchmarks against which solutions were evaluated. The objectives led to a consistent, interrelated system of learning events, including marketing materials, product instructions, and selling techniques.

Exhibit 5-12   Disposition Matrix for the Bed&Body Warmer

	Buyer	User	Reseller
Trash	NA	• Classifies the product as being natural and biodegradable.	NA
Recycle	NA	NA	NA
Sell	NA	NA	• Displays the product attractively. • Identifies customers likely to purchase the product. • Demonstrates the product to customers. • Communicates features and benefits to customers. • Compares the product to competitors. • Answers common customer questions.
Give	• Identifies friends and loved ones who could use the product.	NA	NA

Summary

The key concepts to take away from this chapter include the following:

- Customer education programs relate to the four phases of the comprehensive theory of choice: goal formation, acquisition, consumption, and disposition.
- Goal formation focuses on providing customers the knowledge they need to make a purchase decision. It is tightly linked to the promotion component of the marketing mix.
- Acquisition relates to how customers acquire goods once they have made the purchase decision.
- Consumption involves teaching customers how to use the product. It is linked to the product component of the marketing mix.
- Disposition finds customers trashing, recycling, selling, or giving away products.

The comprehensive theory of choice is the primary means to structure a customer education strategy. One of its benefits is that it maps out the entire relationship with customers and pinpoints the kind of learning they will do at various junctures. Another benefit is that it helps break down what you need to teach customers into logical units that will not overload the customer.

Designing a customer education strategy rests on figuring out what customers need to learn during each of the critical phases. Based on the results of a needs analysis, you construct objectives and relate them to the components of goal formation, acquisition, consumption, and disposition, as well as to the different types of customers. Within the resulting strategy design matrices, the basic plan for your customer education strategy comes alive. Your ultimate task will be to translate these objectives into a complete system of learning events.

Product Systems

The very presence of customer education accompanying a product, whether a manual, videotape, or instructions on the label, indicates that there is a fault with the product. For if products were perfect, there would be no need for customer education or customer support. The product's design would communicate all the customer needed to know for successful understanding and operation.

Door knobs are examples of a product that does not need instruction. Doors do not have signs instructing you how to use the knob. The knob's design is so simple and elegant that it does not require instruction.

The vision that products should not need customer education or customer support is indeed lofty. Most products do need some type of support. Breakthroughs in technology introduce customers to products they have never seen before, that are based on metaphors they have yet to experience. Products might be too complex and overload the cognitive abilities of customers. Facts about products, such as the speed of new computers and the nutritional content of food products, change continually. And because we are human, designing the perfect product is beyond our capabilities. We need to recognize deficiencies in product design and address those deficiencies with support structures, such as customer education and customer support.

Product design and customer support sets a tone for how you need to think about designing customer education. Customer educators do not just create educational events. Rather, they create performance systems that tie together all the elements that contribute to customer success: product design, customer education, and customer support. This product system ensures that customers can understand and use your products successfully. Through a product system strategy, companies can deliver products customers can use effectively, meeting customers' highest expectations. The ultimate result is increased customer satisfaction and a significant competitive advantage.

The Product System

Three components comprise a product system: product design, customer education, and customer support. (See Exhibit 6–1.) A product system for a computer, therefore, includes the ergonomic design of the computer, the instruction manual, and the 800-number telephone support. Alone, a computer is just a product. However, as a simple product system, the solution the customer buys is the sum of the three basic elements. It is the interaction of the system's components that contributes to a customer's success in using the product.

Exhibit 6–1   Theory and Practice of Product Systems

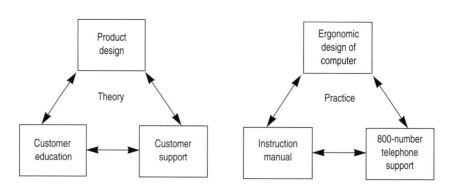

PRODUCT DESIGN

Ergonomics, human factors, man-machine interface, and user interface are sciences that link psychology, physiology, and engineering. In product design, engineers strive to create solutions that address how customers will understand the functions of the product (psychology), as well as how they will manipulate the product (physiology).

Psychological Design. Donald Norman, in his book *The Psychology of Everyday Things,* investigates how humans interact with various objects and products in the world and suggests strategies for the design of easy-to-operate products.[1] The premise of the book is that poor product design causes humans to make mistakes with products. Norman weaves fascinating stories about doors that you pull open, yet have a big flat handle that communicates pushing; faucets that switch the standard design of hot on the left and cold on the right, to hot on the bottom and cold on the top; and heat controls on stoves that do not match the layout of the burner units.

The psychology of product design is cognitive psychology—how people acquire, process, store, and retrieve information. As Norman shows in his research, products communicate with people through their design. And if people are to understand and remember what products are saying, the products' design must fit the way people learn.

Consider how memory affects product design. A person's short-term memory can hold seven plus or minus two chunks of information.[2] If a product design communicates a large sequence of chunks, then it will be difficult for people to understand and use. For example, some television remote controls that have 20 or more buttons are confusing. They have buttons that are all the same size, the same color, and are organized in a very structured fashion. In this type of design, the human mind has difficulty distinguishing the tasks the buttons represent. Other remote controls, however, vary the size of buttons, have asymmetrical button layouts, and use color. (See Exhibit 6–2.) These design elements distinguish one chunk from another. On a Magnavox VCR remote control, large buttons that cut diagonally across the top of the remote control are for tape control—play, stop, fast forward, rewind—and a symmetrical layout of buttons represents channel numbers. Other remote control devices have a door to hide buttons that are infrequently used, which is another way of reducing the information complexity.

Exhibit 6–2   Grouping of Buttons on a Remote Control

Feedback is another psychological aspect of product design. People learn when they understand the results of their actions. When you push a button on a soda machine, the feedback is the delivery of a soda can. This feedback enables you to learn the relationship between the button and the result. If you push the button and do not get a soda can, then you know something is wrong: the machine is broken, you forgot to put in money, or the machine is out of soda. A change in color, sound, tactile expression, or a clear result are all design methods to enhance the feedback a product delivers to customers.

Psychology influences not only the product itself, but also product assembly. A product with many bolts, nuts, washers, and screws results in cognitive overload. This means the task is too much for the mind to process effectively. The complexity arises in part from the need to recognize subtle differences between similar parts, such as a 1/4-inch bolt and a 3/8-inch bolt. To minimize cognitive overload, make sure the product design standardizes parts the customer will assemble. There are complex wood bed frames that use the same type of nuts and bolts for all the linkages. There is no need to teach customers how to distinguish the parts, because they are all the same. As a value-added feature, the frame even comes with the Allen wrench needed to tighten all the nuts and bolts. The whole system makes it easy for customers and ensures their success.

Physiological Design. Whereas psychological design deals with the customer's mind, physiological design focuses on the customer's body. Products must fit the natural constraints our bodies place on them. For example, what if all bowling balls had the same size holes for fingers? For some people, the fit would be just right, and their bowling performance would be excellent. Other people, whose fingers were too small or too large, would not be able to fit them in the bowling ball holes. Their bowling performance would be abysmal.

Physiological design affects not only performance but also people's health. Poorly designed products can cause a variety of health problems, such as cumulative trauma injuries and repetitive stress syndrome. To overcome these health problems, computer manufacturers have redesigned their keyboards, furniture makers now have chairs that adjust in three dimensions, and kitchen tool designers have made handles larger on such products as peelers and spatulas.

Ingersoll-Rand Co. and Group Four Designs teamed to address performance and health issues for Ingersoll-Rand's new line of power tools.[3] The first tool they redesigned was the pneumatic-driven angle wrench. Assembly line workers use angle wrenches to assemble cars, trucks, and tractors.

The first priority the design team had was to understand who was using angle wrenches and how they were using them. To do this, the team visited Chrysler and Caterpillar assembly lines. There they discovered some interesting things. A third of the people on the assembly line were women. This was interesting because tools are typically designed for men, but the average woman's hands are up to two inches smaller than a man's hands. If their hands do not fit the handle of the angle wrench well, it can create health problems for women and reduce the quality of their work.

Other items the design team noticed were the presence of both left- and right-handed people on the assembly line, workers wearing gloves, and tape on the handles. Left-handed people had trouble using the existing wrenches because the wrench controls were designed for right-handed people. The existing angle wrenches had steel handles, so some workers used heavy gloves to keep their hands from getting cold. Other workers wrapped the handle in tape to improve their grip. All of these observations were duly noted by the team and fed into the design process.

The result of this analysis was an angle wrench with a handle whose grip adjusted to three different sizes. Left- and right-handed people could easily operate the forward and reverse controls. A polypropylene handle improved grip and warded off cold. Other design modifications reduced the weight of the angle wrench, improved its balance, and reduced its torque. The result was a tool that Chrysler workers insisted they use and that won a gold medal for best industrial product design from the *Business Week* Annual Design Awards.

CUSTOMER EDUCATION

Much of what we teach customers depends on the product design. Product designs that are easy for customers to interpret require less education. For instance, a graphical user interface on a computer requires less instruction than a command-line interface. Being familiar with the product design and the product development team will help you sense needs that require customer education solutions. Although product design usually drives customer education, there is no reason why customer education cannot drive product design. For instance, you can write instructions for how the product should work first, then design the product based on the instructions. This was done for a retail display made by AuntieA's Inc., the manufacturer of the Bed&Body Warmers described in Chapter 5. The display had many parts, and the position for each part needed to be exact. Otherwise, the display would wobble or collapse, because it held nearly 150 pounds of product. To ensure proper assembly, AuntieA's first wrote the instructions. Then it enhanced the design of the display to follow the instructions exactly, including numbering the major parts in the order of assembly. Exhibit 6–3 shows the two-page instruction sheet.

Writing the instructions first gives you time to clearly think about the processes associated with the product and the knowledge needed to perform those processes. In the example, various problems presented themselves to the writer. For instance, how would the customer distinguish between the four side supports? If they were not marked in some way, the writer would have to devote more space in the instructions to describe a method for distinguishing between the side supports. In this case, enhancing the design reduced the length of the instruction sheets and made the process simpler for the customer.

CUSTOMER SUPPORT

Support refers to a variety of services that help customers use and maintain products. Support ensures that customers can get products fixed when they break and get help when they cannot figure out how to make a feature of the product work. From a usability standpoint, customer support is the last line of defense between a customer's success and failure. If the product design does not communicate with the customer effectively and the customer education does not stimulate learning, the customer needs someone who can help immediately. Put another way, customers need someone to hold their hands.

You might think customer support and customer education are synonymous. In some ways they are. Contacting a customer service rep can often provide you with the knowledge and skills you need. Customer education is primarily proactive, in that it defines what customers need and delivers the knowledge and skills to them. Customer support, on the other hand, is primarily reactive. Customer support kicks in when neither the design of the product nor the manual solves the customer's problem.

For instance, a manual might not cover or completely explain specific tasks that customers want to perform. Customers who discover major defects with a product require direct interaction with a company representative to get the problem fixed. Also, customer support motivates customers and provides services product design and customer training ignore. The typical form of customer support is the toll-free 800 telephone number. If you have a problem using the product, call the 800-number and a customer or technical support person will help you resolve the problem. If you sell product retail, you should be prepared for customers to come to the store seeking help. The same is true if you provide house calls through a field service organization.

Exhibit 6–3   Display Assembly Instructions

Assembly Instructions
48-unit Retail Display

Parts

Before you start assembly, check that you have these parts:

1   Angled top box
1   Straight middle box
1   Large bottom box
4   Side supports
1   Acrylic placard with color poster
24 Long wood screws for side supports (Harry, our carpenter, sometimes uses more)
2   Short wood screws for acrylic placard (already set in the angled top box)

Installation Tools

- Phillips head screwdriver
  (Note: A phillips head drill bit and drill will speed up the assembly task)

Assembly Procedure

1. Lay the boxes on their sides on the floor so the pre-drilled screw holes face up. You should see labels next to each drill hole: The angled top box has A1 and B1, the straight middle box has A2 and B2, and the large bottom box has A3 and B3. If you see C and D labels on a box, turn the box over so the A and B labels are on top.

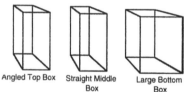

Angled Top Box   Straight Middle   Large Bottom
                        Box   Box

2. Match the A and B side supports to the boxes. For example, A1 on the side support should match A1 on the top box, A2 on the side support should match A2 on the middle box, and A3 on the side support should match A3 on the bottom box.

3. Screw the side supports to the boxes.

April 1, 1996   AuntieA's, Inc. PO Box 6255 Reno, NV 89513 702-747-4828   Page 1 of 2

4. Flip the display so the attached side supports are on the floor and the C and D labels are visible. Assemble the C and D side supports the same way as you did in steps 2 and 3.

5. With all four side supports installed, stand the display upright.

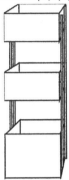

6. Attach the acrylic placard to the back of the angled top box. To do this, unscrew the two small screws, align the acrylic placard with the holes, then screw the two small screws through the holes in the acrylic placard into the box.

7. Find a good location for the display then fill it with Bed&Body Warmers. Remember that with 48 units, the display will weigh nearly 150 pounds. So don't try and move it when filled!

Does your display look like this?

If you have any problems with assembly, please call Peter or Beth at 702-747-4828. We're more than happy to help.

A new trend in customer support is on-line support through the customer's computer. Computer and software companies have been doing this for years, through bulletin board services (BBS). In this model, a customer can e-mail a company with a question or search through the company's database of customer support issues and solutions. For example, America OnLine (AOL) offers a Tech Support Live service to aid customers who have problems using AOL. (See Exhibit 6–4.) To use the service, users log into one of several tech support chat rooms. Users are helped by the AOL technician in the order that they entered the chat room. While you wait to be called, you see the questions other users have and the responses of the AOL technician. When it is your turn, the AOL technician asks what your question is. You type it in the field at the bottom of the screen, then click the Chat In Row button. Your question appears in the list, and moments later the AOL technician will answer your question.

Many companies maintain message boards on on-line services such as AOL to provide support services. On these message boards, users seek help not only from the company, but also from other users. The message board shown in Exhibit 6–5 is for Global Village

Exhibit 6–4 America OnLine Tech Support Live Chat Session

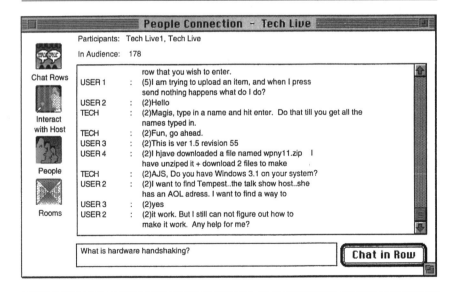

Exhibit 6-5   Message Board in America OnLine

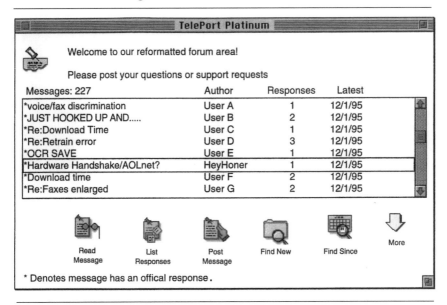

Exhibit 6-6   Message Posted on the Message Board

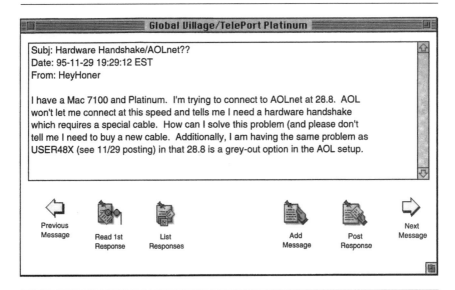

Exhibit 6-7   Reply from Global Village Technical Support

Communications, a maker of computer modems. It lists all the questions and support requests submitted by users of the TelePort Platinum modem. Exhibits 6–6 and 6–7 show a customer's support request and an answer to the support request from a Global Village technical support person.

One problem in any customer support endeavor is the ability of the technical support specialist to decipher what customers are asking. If products have confusing terminology and parts that are not clearly labeled, any communication between customer and support specialist, whether on-line or over the phone, will be difficult. For instance, if the customer does not know the name of the part, he or she will make up a name for it or attempt to describe it. This only makes matters worse for both the customer and the support specialist as they both try to figure out what the other is saying. Product design and customer education must ensure that customers and support specialists can speak the same language and easily identify product parts. This means that product parts must be clearly and consistently identified on both the product and in the educational materials.

INTERACTION BETWEEN THE ELEMENTS

As the complexity of products increase, the demand for customer education and support increases as well. The premise of a product system is that the less user-friendly a product is, the more customer education and support are required. Additionally, if the customer education is poor, the quality of customer support must be high.

Product systems is a model for both design and operations. As a design model, it helps you structure your product development process and product teams to ensure you build a system of solutions, not just a box. As an operations model, product systems help you predict and plan your resources for supporting a product. Products will ship with flaws in their design, either in the product itself or in the supporting systems. Recognizing these flaws will help you plan the training for your customer support reps as well as customer service staffing needs.

Examples of Product Systems

As a consumer in today's marketplace, you have no doubt experienced product systems of varying quality. This section discusses three product systems that offer exceptional models for practice: the ProStep nicotine patch, Macintosh computers, and JBL's SoundEffects stereo speaker system.

PROSTEP

A pharmaceutical industry conference on patient information and education featured the ProStep system as a best practice for patient education. However, the ProStep system goes beyond just education; it is an excellent example of a well-designed product system. ProStep is a nicotine patch marketed by Lederle Labs that patients use to quit smoking. Patients stick the patch on their arm, and it slowly releases nicotine through the skin into the blood stream. The nicotine from the patch replaces the nicotine smokers get from cigarettes, reducing the physiological need to smoke. However, smoking is as much psychological as it is physiological. Getting people off cigarettes for good requires a multi-dimensional approach.

First, the ProStep patch has wonderful ergonomics. What could be simpler than sticking a patch to your upper arm as a way to taking medicine? There are no pills, no shots, and no creams. Second, customer education is quite extensive. When prescribed ProStep, patients get an enrollment kit. This kit includes not only instructions for the product, but also pamphlets and materials to aid in supporting the patient's commitment to smoking cessation. These materials inform the patient about referral organizations and give behavior modification tips. The kit also contains a sponge ball for patients to squeeze when their craving for nicotine makes them anxious. Third, there is an innovative customer support program. Patients can call one 800-number to get product and referral information (e.g., the location of the closest smoking cessation program), and another 800-number connects the patient to a smoking cessation specialist who will try to help the patient find ways of not smoking.

ProStep's aim is to get people off cigarettes. However, they recognized that the nicotine patch was not a miracle cure. To ensure that the product achieved its aim, Lederle incorporated education and support components to address the psychological aspects of smoking cessation.

MACINTOSH

The Macintosh computer is another example of a product system. When the first Macintosh arrived on the scene in 1984, it was a revolutionary jump in human-computer interaction. The Macintosh system software design, where users manipulate objects with a mouse instead of typing commands, brought computing in line with how we work in the real world. In addition to the software, Macintosh hardware maintains this easy-to-use design philosophy. Apple advertisements in the fall of 1992 identified DOS-based and Windows-based systems as "the hard way," where every upgrade to the computer requires an extensive system reconfiguration. (Windows 95 overcame these problems with its plug-and-play technology.) The ad goes on to show the Macintosh as "the easy way," where built-in features cause upgrades to require little or no system reconfiguration, and if reconfiguration is necessary, the process is extraordinarily simple.

The training components of the Macintosh system are also impressive. As soon as a customer opens the box, the packaging leads him through the process of setting up and using the computer with documents labeled "Read This First," "Read This Second," and "Read This Third." A software-based interactive guided tour teaches the customer how to use the mouse and perform basic functions, and a well-written set of product documentation and manuals supports additional learning.

Apple historically handled customer support through its network of resellers, but the introduction of PowerBook computers in the early 1990s saw the birth of an 800-number to help customers with technical problems. Through this number, PowerBook owners could talk to an Apple technical support engineer to solve problems or to arrange for product repair. Apple has now expanded 800-number customer support to cover all Apple products.

JBL SOUNDEFFECTS SPEAKER SYSTEM

Stereo speakers are not complex pieces of technology from a user interface standpoint. Whereas a computer requires a user interface design to facilitate constant interaction with a user, speakers require little or no attention beyond plugging them in. But plugging in stereo speakers can often be a problem, especially when the speaker cables need to run under carpets or through walls. To overcome this problem, JBL introduced a wireless technology that made it easier for customers to install the speakers. A central RF transmitter plugs into a stereo amplifier. The transmitter broadcasts a signal to a receiver connected to the speakers. Through this design, the customer can position the speakers anywhere within range of the transmitter. This technology simplified the setup task.

JBL partnered with Fitch, Inc., a product design firm, to design the product system. The customer education part of the SoundEffects line has both pre-sale and post-sale elements. The pre-sale element consists primarily of product packaging and point-of-purchase displays that enable customers to configure their speaker system correctly. Product boxes feature prominent numbers to indicate related components. (See Exhibit 6–8.) For example, number 1 reflects components for home theater, and number 2 reflects components for music. Thus, customers could easily recognize the components they should not mix. The point-of-purchase displays introduced customers to the wireless technology, providing information about how it works.

Given the distribution channel for the speakers (superstores and warehouse clubs), providing pre-sales education was important. In these stores, customers make buying decisions without much help from a salesperson. Additionally, salespeople are responsible for a much

Exhibit 6–8   SoundEffects Product Line

Exhibit 6–9   SoundEffects Instruction Sheet

Photos: Peter Rice, Boston. Courtesy of SoundEffects and Fitch, Inc.

wider array of products. Thus, the packaging and point-of-purchase display must enable the customer to make an informed choice as well as act as sales aids for the salesperson.

Post-sale customer education consists of a single instruction sheet. Its design reflects the style and image of the product line, and it clearly communicates an incredibly simple set of instructions. (See Exhibit 6–9.) Using lighthearted cartoons and clear product illustrations, the instruction sheet leads the customer through four steps. It starts with ensuring all contents are in the box, continues with providing ideas for where to position the speakers and making connections to the amplifier and receiver, and concludes with balancing the speakers for optimum surround sound. The instructions are in plain English, all the way down to the technical specifications (affectionately referred to as "Arts and Sciences").

Both an 800-number and a referral to the customer's dealer are the two customer support solutions that accompany the SoundEffects line. What is interesting about the customer support is that the referral for customer support is in plain view at the top of the instruction sheet. This is in contrast with other instruction sheets and manuals that bury the customer support number in a paragraph at the end. JBL clearly recognizes that customer support is an important part of the product system. It should be easy for customers to locate the number.

For all three product systems, the design of the system focuses on the interaction between product design, customer education, and customer support. Well-designed products and extensive education and training materials eliminate most customer problems. Customer support catches problems that slip through and provides an additional level of service that ergonomics and training just cannot meet.

Strategies for Product Systems Design

Designing effective product systems requires an appreciation of the dynamic interaction between product design, education, and support. Each component is dependent on the others, and the failure of any one results in the failure of the whole system. The less user-friendly a product is, the more customer training and customer support are required. Customer support must be intensive if the quality of customer training is low.

Traditionally, companies design product systems from the product down. First, the engineers design the product. Next, an instructional designer or technical writer is brought in to figure out what customers need to learn and how to teach them. Once the product and the education are complete, the customer support department prepares its database and trains people in how to support the product. The result, of course, is a product system.

While logical in approach, this design methodology is limited in actual practice. The problem is timing. Waiting to bring instructional designers and technical writers in until the product is nearly complete is counterproductive. The process of writing instructions for a product does wonders for a product's design. For instance, if procedures are too long and complicated, then perhaps a redesign of the product will make the procedure shorter, hence easier for customers to use and understand. The same holds true for customer support personnel. Who better to include on a design team than the people who talk with customers every day, who understand the customers' needs? The best product systems, therefore, are the result of user-centered design and multifaceted teams.

USER-CENTERED DESIGN

User-centered design focuses product design decisions on the needs of the user. There is always the risk that technology will overwhelmingly drive product design, resulting in products that are technological wonders but of little use to the targeted customers. User-centered design balances technology with the psychology and physiology of people. As Donald Norman so simply phrases it, the outcome of user-centered design is to "make sure that (1) the user can figure out what to do, and (2) the user can tell what is going on."[4]

User-centered design starts with knowing your users. The design team from Ingersoll-Rand and Group Four Design learned about its customers by visiting assembly lines. This knowledge translated into radical new product designs that fit the needs of a male and female work force. Similarly, employees from 3M have visited operating rooms to see how physicians use 3M's medical products. Such customer insight enabled the employees to conceive of new packaging schemes that enable physicians to more easily open sterile packages while wearing rubber gloves. In both of these cases, the aim is for the product to fit the natural elements of the user's work, rather than modifying the work to fit the product.

Once you know who your users are and the tasks they must accomplish, you can start designing. Norman prescribes seven key principles for user-centered design.[5]

Use Both Knowledge in the World and Knowledge in the Head. Knowledge in the world are artifacts and cues that indicate the purpose of a device, like the lettered keys on a keyboard. Knowledge in the head is memory, such as knowing what the letter "T" represents and knowing what will happen when you push the letter "T" on a keyboard. Good product systems harmonize the cues people need to understand actions and outcomes, with the knowledge needed to act and interpret. However, a product can only take the user part of the way. Customer education must fill in the gaps.

Simplify the Structure of Tasks. If a complicated product cannot be modified, there are other strategies to simplify the tasks. Memory aids, such as quick reference cards or a mousepad that list F-key commands, can support and streamline performance. You can also automate part of the task to make it easier for the user. Technology can often improve the human interaction with a product. Velcro fasteners on shoes make the task of tying shoelaces unnecessary and change the meaning of tying shoes.

Make Things Visible. If users cannot see the relationship between their actions with products and the effects of those actions, then the product is not usable. Results of actions need to be visible and intuitive, like when you flip on a light switch and the lights come on. There must be a direct cause-and-effect relationship that the user can observe and understand.

Get the Mappings Right. Mappings relate physical objects to our mental structures and expectations. A door with a large flat handle communicates to users that they must push the door to open it. If the door operates that way, the mapping is right. However, if the door only opens if the user pulls the handle, the mapping is wrong. The same is true for controls for home appliances. To effectively use a stove, the burner controls must map to the position of the burners. For example, the left rear control must control the left rear burner. However, if the arrangement of burner controls is in a line, it is difficult to know which control controls which burner. In this case, the mappings are wrong causing user confusion. (See Exhibit 6–10.)

Exhibit 6–10   Good and Poor Control Mapping

Good Mapping	Poor Mapping
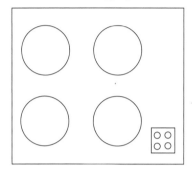	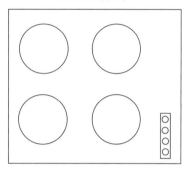
The relationships of the controls maps to the position of the burners.	The relationship of the controls does not map to the position of the burners.

Source: Adapted from Donald A. Norman, *The Psychology of Everyday Things* (New York: Basic Books, 1988).

Exploit the Power of Constraints, Both Natural and Artificial. The simplest of aptitude tests requires subjects to fit specifically shaped objects through a complementary hole. Square peg goes into the square hole, round peg into the round hole, and so on. The constraint for the task is geometry: square pegs will not fit in the round holes. And trying to force it will eventually cause something to break.

If your product requires assembly, think about how you can establish constraints to ensure successful assembly. Some computers have different types of connectors to make different types of connections. The connector for attaching a hard drive is different from the connector for attaching the keyboard. The different connectors help the user make the decision about what goes together. Make sure that things that should not go together cannot be forced together. Remember, you never want a customer to force a square peg in the round hole.

Product operations also require constraints. Industrial equipment has devices call interlocks that prevent users from accessing dangerous areas of the product while it is operating. For example, a product such as a DNA sequencer uses a laser beam to read data from samples. Users need to be protected from exposure to the laser beam, which can cause blindness. Thus, interlocks make sure the user cannot open the cover of the product while it is in operation.

Design for Error. People are not perfect. They will make mistakes and they will want to recover from those mistakes without much pain. If possible, your product design should enable users to reverse actions or warn users of destructive actions. Software applications design for error by having an Undo command. The Undo command reverses the outcome of the last user event. Thus, if you accidentally hit a button that erases your monthly report, you just choose Undo and the computer corrects your mistake.

When All Else Fails, Standardize. If none of the previously described principles offers a solution to your design problem, then you will have to find your own solution. The caveat, however, is that once you choose a solution, that solution becomes a standard for future solutions. For example, once the decision was made in the United States that automobiles drive on the right side of the road, it had to stay that way. If states or cities arbitrarily decided whether their community would support right-side driving or left-side driving, there would be mass confusion every time drivers crossed the state line or city limits.

MULTIFACETED TEAMS

The composition of the most basic multifaceted team for creating product systems draws people from product design, customer education, and customer support. A simple product system team typically includes an engineer, a writer, and a customer service specialist. Each of these people has a unique set of skills and knowledge to build the system. The engineer has the skills to make the product. The writer has skills to teach people to use the product. And the customer service specialist has the skills to help and reassure customers over the phone or in person.

During the design process, the team works together to create solutions and resolve design problems. As the engineer creates product designs, the writer looks at the designs and thinks about how easy it is to write instructions for the design. If the design is too difficult to explain with words, then the writer recommends to the engineer ideas that simplify the design to simplify instructions. Similarly, the customer service specialist looks at the design in terms of how easy it is to talk the customer through a problem over the phone. Product parts that look similar but perform different tasks might need to look more dissimilar so a customer support person can clearly communicate instructions to the customer. The customer service specialist also reviews the writer's work to make sure there are instructions and explanations that address common customer questions.

But as product systems become more complex, so does the composition of the team. The product design part of the team can grow to include scientists, industrial designers, manufacturing engineers, purchasing agents, cognitive psychologists, and ergonomists. The customer education contingent can include graphic designers, instructional designers, and trainers. The customer support group can include salespeople and service technicians. Other potential team members that provide strategy and guidance throughout the design process include marketers, product managers, market researchers, and even customers. Exhibit 6–11 lists the various product systems team members and their typical contributions to the product development process.

Exhibit 6–11 Common Product System Team Members and Their Roles

Cognitive psychologist	Provides information on how to improve the customer's psychological interaction with products.
Customer	Provides information about customer needs and whether the product resolves those needs.
Customer support specialist	Provides information about customer problems and needs based on communications with customers. Looks at the product design and customer education from the standpoint of the kinds of calls they will cause.
Engineer	Provides skills that manipulate various physical and technological elements to make the product work. Depending on the project, the team might include software, hardware, electrical, and mechanical engineers.
Ergonomist	Provides information on how to improve the customer's physical interaction with the product.
Graphic designer	Provides visual design skills to create displays and visual elements of the product, as well as the graphic design of customer education materials.
Instructional designer	Provides the skills to design the customer education component of the product system.
Industrial designer	Provides three-dimensional design skills to fashion the overall look and feel of the product.
Manufacturing engineer	Provides insight on whether the product design can be manufactured in the necessary quantities at the necessary price.

Exhibit 6-11   Cont'd.

Marketer/product manager	Provides the product features the product should have to meet the customers' needs as well as the strategy for marketing the product.
Market researcher	Provides information on customer demographics, customer needs, and performance of past products.
Salesperson	Provides information on the needs of customers and ideas for how the product design can facilitate an efficient sales pitch.
Scientist	Provides the basic concept or core technology of the product.
Service technician	Provides information on how customers are using the product in the field. Helps identify customer needs, gaps in the product system, and misuse areas.
Purchasing agent	Provides skills to ensure that raw materials for the product design are available at a specific price.
Trainer	Provides information on how easy it is to teach customers how to use a product.
Writer	Provides the skills to write about the product, whether instructions or promotion. Includes creative writers, public relations writers, and technical writers.

Fitch, Inc., the product design firm that worked on the SoundEffects speaker line, uses multifaceted teams for all its design projects. In the case of the SoundEffects project, product designers, engineers, industrial designers, graphic designers, and technical writers formed the team early in the design process. This ensured that the theme and vision driving the design touched all of the elements that the customer would see, from the aesthetic design of the speakers to the instruction sheet. The aim is consistency of communication. On other Fitch projects, such as its redesign of the 3M videotape product line, people from manufacturing and purchasing join the core design team to balance the creative design with the real-world needs of retooling assembly lines and acquiring raw materials.

Summary

The key points to remember from this chapter include the following:

- A product system consists of product design, customer education, and customer support elements.
- The interaction between the elements contributes to usability. A well-designed product with appropriate customer education and customer support will enable customers to use the product successfully.
- The primary strategies for developing product systems are user-centered design and multifaceted teams.

Not every product requires a product system. Some products, such as Post-It Notes, utensils, and light switches, are so intuitive that extensive education or support insults the intelligence of the customer and wastes the company's money. The art of designing product systems is recognizing the gaps that exist between product design, education, and support, and balancing those gaps with the needs of customers. Customers who can use your products efficiently and effectively will be satisfied customers. And their satisfaction does not just stop there. Their loyalty to your company will increase, and they will tell their friends about their satisfaction with the product.

Customer
Education
Solutions

Once a company analyzes customer needs and structures an education program, the customer education design must be implemented. The company must establish the curriculum, design training courses, and write instruction manuals. In short, the company will develop a comprehensive customer education program by selecting specific instructional techniques and tactics, establishing the sequence for instruction, applying instructional methods, and choosing the appropriate media to carry the instruction.

This chapter presents case studies examining how five organizations—Pfizer Animal Health, Charles Schwab & Co., 3M, Safety-Kleen, and Hewlett-Packard—have created customer education solutions for a variety of opportunities and situations. As you read these case studies, reflect on how these companies have incorporated the various customer education strategies and methods discussed in previous chapters.

Pfizer Animal Health's Handle with Care Program

In 1991, the U.S. beef processing industry had losses of nearly $700 million due to animal mishandling. As cattle move from feedstock through feedlot and processor to consumer, numerous factors can reduce the quality of the beef. Injections of antibiotics while the cattle are in the field or at the feedlot can cause blemishes in the beef, improper transportation can cause sickness among the cattle, and improper storage of the beef after processing can promote the growth of harmful bacteria.

It was the antibiotics problem that concerned Pfizer Animal Health. In 1990, Pfizer learned that its line of Ultrabac® vaccines caused blemishes when handlers injected the vaccine into cattle. These blemishes did not affect the safety of the beef, but they did affect how the U.S. Department of Agriculture (USDA) graded it. A drop in USDA grade meant a drop in price. The blemish problem had two possible effects: it could reduce the overall demand for beef and it could reduce the demand for Pfizer's cornerstone animal vaccine.

The solution to Pfizer's problem was relatively simple. If cattle handlers changed the location of the injection from the rear end to the neck, it would eliminate blemishes. Yet cattle handlers had always injected cattle in the rear end. Thus, the challenge presented to Pfizer was to teach cattle handlers a new method for injecting cattle and to ensure acceptance of the new method.

PROGRAM

The first phase of the Handle with Care program focused on educating processing crews and pen riders in the feedlot sector of the beef producing market. When cattle arrive at the feedlot, their processing includes vaccine injections to prevent sickness and disease from spreading throughout the herd. This sector caused few of the mishandling problems, but its small size (approximately 200 feedlots) made changing existing handling practices easier. It was the best place to test the Handle with Care program.

Working in conjunction with the National Cattlemen's Association and the Academy of Veterinary Consultants, Pfizer's customer education strategy was to equip its sales force, as well as state cattle associations and beef quality assurance task forces, with a high-quality and adaptable set of educational materials. Pfizer also changed the instructions on Ultrabac product labels to specify a neck injection rather than a rear-end injection. Salespeople could use these materials for formal presentations as well as chuteside product demonstrations. The materials Pfizer developed included the following:

- A 22-minute video entitled, "A Guide to Wholesome Beef Production"
- A slide show/script version of the video that salespeople could use for customer presentations
- A "Processing Points" wall chart that diagrams where cattle should receive injections
- A take-home brochure
- Stuffers
- Processing maps to help document the vaccines each steer receives
- Chuteside demonstration cards that depict the process for giving cattle injections of Ultrabac

The chuteside demonstration was a popular and successful learning activity. Chutes are the labyrinths of steel gates used to move cattle from one place to another. Within a series of chutes, there is typically a squeeze chute. The squeeze chute temporarily halts an animal's movement through the chutes by squeezing the animal between two gates. With the animal restrained in the squeeze chute, a Pfizer salesperson gives a live demonstration of how to administer the Ultrabac product. The salesperson describes why the injection should occur in the neck rather than the rear end, identifies the best place for the injection, then injects the animal with the vaccine. During this demonstration, the salesperson also details various facts about the Ultrabac product and answers questions from the cattle handlers. The salesperson also shows how the cattle handlers can use the processing map Pfizer provides to record the injections, ensuring that they will comply with the recommended Ultrabac regimen.

The success of the Handle with Care program in the feedlot sector pushed Pfizer to adapt the program to the cow-calf sector. This sector comprises a large number of independent cattle ranchers. They then sell the cattle to stockers and feedlots. In contrast to the feedlot sector, mishandling problems in the cow-calf sector exists in the field and on the range. Getting the message out and ensuring that ranchers are compliant is difficult.

To address the needs of this marketplace, Pfizer developed two new elements in its existing program: a 20-minute video entitled "Quality Beef Begins with You" and a companion, take-home brochure. Pfizer salespeople and state cattle associations could use these materials during cattle raising meetings and visits to ranches.

RESULTS

The Handle with Care program delivered several important results for Pfizer Animal Health:

- By the end of 1991,40 states had ordered Handle with Care program materials. This positioned Pfizer as the leading industry ally in the beef quality assurance effort.
- The Handle with Care program reduced the number of blemishes found in beef. Data from the National Cattlemen's Association showed that blemishes fell 12 percent over a two-year period. (See Exhibit 7–1.) This reduction accounts for nearly $15 million in avoided losses.
- The Handle with Care program contributed to increased sales and new business. Sales of Ultrabac doubled over a five-year period from the time Pfizer introduced the Handle with Care program. (See Exhibit 7–2.)

Charles Schwab & Co.

For more than 20 years, Charles Schwab & Co. has been a leading discount broker. As a broker, Schwab helps investors buy and sell stocks, bonds, mutual funds, and other investments. Schwab is different from other full-service brokers, such as Merrill Lynch and Payne Webber, in that its customer service representatives (what the other brokerages call account executives) do not receive commissions on customer transactions. Schwab representatives also do not advise customers or recommend specific investments. Schwab's aim is to serve self-directed investors, people who want to do investment research and make investment decisions on their own.

When Schwab first began serving customers, it did nothing more than process customer orders. However, as the market for discount brokerages matured and more customers brought their investments to

Exhibit 7–1   Reduction of Beef Blemishes over Two Years

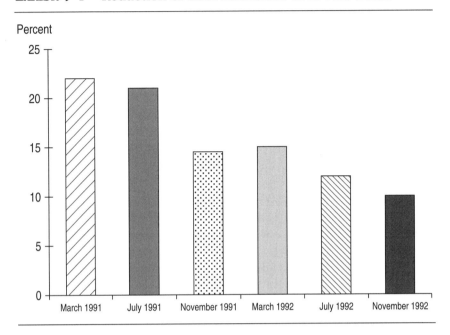

Exhibit 7–2   Sales of Ultrabac during the Handle with Care Program

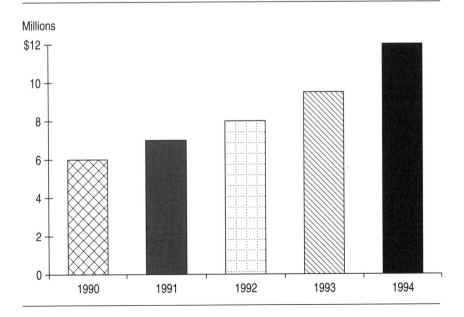

Schwab, Schwab noticed opportunities for building strong relationships with its customers through customer education. Even though the typical Schwab customer is self-directed, these customers still seek knowledge and skills to make better investment decisions. For example, the booming mutual fund marketplace has made the task of selecting a mutual fund a daunting process. Schwab itself represents 900 different mutual funds. Through its branches, Schwab learned that customers needed help in sorting through the various options, while still making their own decision.

Yet the investment knowledge and skills Schwab customers have is radically divergent. Some new customers cannot tell the difference between a stock and a mutual fund. A 1994 Schwab survey revealed that 50 percent of new customers had never had an investment relationship with a brokerage. Other customers have years of experience playing the market and seek out specific information to help them make wise investment decisions.

Schwab gets ideas for customer education solutions through its branch offices and telephone customer service representatives. A customer might mention an idea to a representative, or the representative might notice specific needs. These ideas move up through the organization to a marketing group. This group assesses the feasibility of ideas. If an idea passes muster, someone will champion the idea and try to get it approved and funded by management. The development of Schwab's customer education solutions is then handled by its corporate communications department.

PROGRAMS

To meet divergent customer needs, Schwab has several educational programs for customers. These include seminars, printed materials, and third-party information. Seminars focus on broad, popular topics. Printed materials provide details on various aspects of investing. And third-party information serves the needs of sophisticated investors.

Seminars. Schwab seminars are held in Schwab branch offices around the country. The seminars focus on various topics, such as mutual fund investing, retirement investing, and on-line investing. The seminars are aimed toward the novice investor and are publicized in local publications and direct-mail packages.

Seminars are led by branch personnel. The design of the seminar and the materials for the seminar are developed at the corporate office.

This ensures that each Schwab branch delivers a consistent presentation to customers and that the content within the seminar meets Securities Exchange Commission and National Association of Securities Dealers regulations. Schwab teaches branch personnel the content for the course as well as how to deliver the course through Schwab University, its in-house employee training department.

Schwab seminars are heavy on content, but the seminar design also ensures that there is plenty of time for customers to ask questions. Schwab found that the question-and-answer session following the seminar was customers' favorite activity.

Self-Paced Printed Materials. For customers who cannot attend the seminars, Schwab offers various self-paced materials to build customer knowledge and skills in a variety of areas. In addition to its Mutual Fund Selection Planner™ (see Exhibit 5–3), Schwab has guides for various investment topics and Schwab products. Its "Guide to Investing" covers investing basics, asset categories, and asset allocations. The "Guide to Using TeleBroker®" teaches customers how to use Schwab's 24-hour, telephone-based, automated brokerage service.

Third-Party Information. As a company familiar with the brokerage industry, Schwab is in a unique position to serve as a conduit to distribute investment reports and research to customers. Sophisticated investors need detailed information about the performance of investments, the financial position of publicly traded companies, and market trends.

Schwab is an expert at acquiring, managing, and organizing investment information from a variety of third parties, and it passes that expertise along to customers in the form of research and monitoring reports. As a Schwab customer, you can get Morningstar mutual fund reports, company research reports, and Standard & Poor's five-star stock lists. Through Schwab's Research on Request™ service, you can get other third-party research reports, news articles, and price charts on thousands of companies. Schwab makes getting the information easy: a phone call is all it takes to request the information, and most items are free. The fees for other items are minimal.

Aside from the specific programs it provides, Schwab strives to promote a learning environment in everything it does. When you call a Schwab representative or visit a Schwab branch, Schwab sees it as an opportunity for you to learn something about investing. Schwab's systems are designed to facilitate an open exchange of ideas. Its policy of no employee commissions on customer trades reinforces the theme that all the information you will get from Schwab is free from bias.

RESULTS

Schwab expects its customer education systems to provide results. Although the seminars are occasions for customers to learn, Schwab expects that attendance at seminars will translate into new accounts and more frequent trades. Here is one of Schwab's measures of success. In the 12 months between October 1994 and October 1995, Schwab increased its client equity by $52 billion, to $172 billion. (See Exhibit 7–3.) Some of this increase is attributed to market factors, but Schwab reports that a significant proportion of the increase stems from new accounts and account transfers. Schwab believes that investors "vote with their dollars," and the increase in client equity reflects the success of the way Schwab does business—Helping Investors Help Themselves.™

In addition to increases in client equity, Schwab assesses the success of its customer education programs by the number of people who attend seminars or order educational materials, and by how many of

Exhibit 7–3 Increase in Schwab's Client Equity over One Year

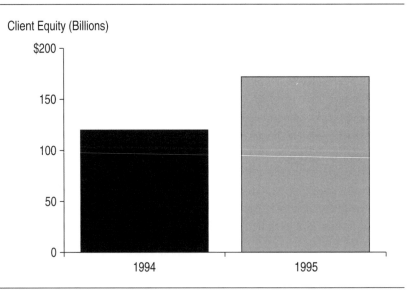

those people actually choose to open an account, place a trade, or request additional information. One Schwab success story is a 14-year-old Florida boy who has been in charge of investing his college fund since age 10. He researches investments, charts their progress, and directs his parents to make trades. (He is under 18, so he cannot execute the trades himself.) A lot of what he knows about investing comes from Schwab's customer education programs. So far, the kid's investment savvy has translated into a small fortune of $60,000. [1]

3M (Minnesota Mining and Manufacturing): Occupational Health and Environmental Safety Division

3M is in many diverse businesses, from adhesives such as tape, glues, and Post-It Notes®, to audio and video recording tapes. Its Occupational Health and Environmental Safety Division (OH&ESD) markets a variety of health and safety products, such as respirators, hearing protection products, substances to absorb chemical spills, slip-resistant matting, and reflective vests. The customer education strategy discussed here focuses on 3M's respirator products, which are worn over the face to prevent harmful airborne particles from entering the lungs.

Over 20 years in the respirator business, 3M has seen sales grow and products change due to numerous federal and state health regulations that require workers to wear respirators on the job. 3M fell into providing customers education solutions for respirators when a 1980 survey found that decision makers wanted 3M to make their job easier in terms of the regulatory and training issues surrounding respirators. Increased workplace injuries due to improperly used and maintained respirators and related workers' compensation claims were also a driving force toward customer education.

PROGRAMS

The 3M sales force recognized that an educational system was a good way to build customer relationships. 3M sales representatives soon found themselves spending 30 to 40 percent of their time training end users. As 3M became more sophisticated in its educational systems, the OH&ESD formed an end-user training committee consisting of marketing communications, technical services, and sales training staff to develop new educational programs.

New programs had to fit the many types of customers in the distribution chain for respirator products: distributors, safety distributors, and end users. Distributors and safety distributors needed to know how to sell the right piece of equipment for the right application. End users needed to know how to use and maintain the respirators, as well as how to teach fellow employees how to use the respirators.

Distributor Seminars. 3M sponsors a special series of seminars for distributors called Horizons. For these seminars, 3M invites only distributors who meet specific performance criteria including sales increases, new business, sponsorship of product sales meetings, participation in OH&ESD promotions, and cooperation on joint sales calls with 3M sales representatives. Selected distributors attend the seminars free of charge—3M even picks up travel expenses and most meals. The Horizon seminars cover product training, total value selling, and leadership and performance coaching:

- **Product training.** This four-day seminar provides hands-on experiences with 3M OH&ESD products. Included in the seminar are presentations by 3M technical staff, presentations of new applications for 3M products, and presentations highlighting the marketing opportunity for 3M products.
- **Total value selling.** This three-day seminar develops distributor sales skills. Topics include how to plan sales calls, determining customer needs, selling your company's "total value," overcoming resistance, and gaining customer commitment. The seminar uses practice sessions and role playing to help distributors learn and practice these new sales skills.
- **Leadership and performance coaching.** This three-day seminar is aimed at supervisors of salespeople within the distributor's organization. The seminar teaches supervisors how to lead and motivate their sales force.

End-User Seminars. 3M provides end users of respirator products two kinds of seminars. The formal professional/technical development programs help customers learn how to set up, manage, maintain, and monitor a respiratory protection program, and workshops conducted by 3M sales representatives help the customer's employees learn how to use and maintain 3M respirators. 3M also offers train-the-trainer workshops where selected customer employees become certified to teach other employees to use and maintain respirators.

Through the professional/technical development program, customers can also earn continuing education units through affiliated colleges, as well as credits through professional associations. Seminars within the program are held several times throughout the year in various locations. The seminars in the program cover respiratory protection, respirator maintenance, exposure assessment, respirator selection, and respirator program development in a series of courses ranging from one to four and a half days long.

Collateral Materials. In addition to the seminars, 3M offers customers a variety of collateral training materials to supplement in-house training and 3M seminars. These materials consist primarily of videotapes and posters covering product selection, product fitting, and reasons for use. (See Exhibit 7–4.) Customers can use these materials to lead their own training programs for employees or to provide employees with self-paced, individualized instruction. Other materials include respirator selection guides that enable customers to match the airborne contaminants found in the workplace with the correct 3M respirator and two interactive, computer programs:

- 3M Select Software helps customers select the right respirator for the needs of the workplace.
- 3M Compliance Software helps customers manage their respiratory protection program in compliance with Occupational Safety and Health Administration (OSHA) requirements. It provides a number of forms to document the program and alerts customers when employees need refresher training and fit tests. (See Exhibit 7–5.)

Sales Force Training. Because the sales force is instrumental in delivering customer education, 3M has an extensive training program called Discovery, which ensures that all sales representatives have the necessary knowledge and skills to effectively communicate with and teach customers. In addition to the typical sales training courses that include sales communication skills and resource management, Discovery includes an extensive curriculum of technical and product training courses including Environmental Safety, Industrial Hygiene and Regulation, Respiratory Products, and the Respiratory Protection Program.

**Exhibit 7–4   Collateral Materials for 3M Respirator Training:
Videos, Posters, and Selection Guides**

Courtest of 3M Occupational Health and Environmental Safety Division.

RESULTS

OH&ESD's customer education strategy accounts for three primary results:

- Resolving an important customer need in the marketplace
- Stimulating double-digit growth in U.S. operations since the inception of the strategy
- Stimulating 50 percent growth in sales in international markets where 3M has introduced the customer education strategy

By the end of 1995, 3M had trained over 20,000 supervisors who, in turn, trained one million end users of respiratory products. To 3M's surprise, many competitors have not established comparative education

Exhibit 7–5   Screen from 3M Compliance Software Demo Disk

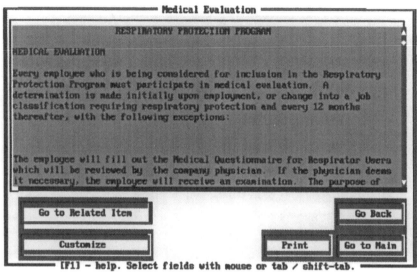

Courtest of 3M Occupational Health and Environmental Safety Division.

programs for customers. 3M speculates that they are discouraged by the potential liability associated with providing the training.

OH&ESD sales representatives pride themselves on being able to provide customer education wherever and whenever it is needed. When a terrorist bomb destroyed the Alfred P. Murrah Federal Building in Oklahoma City in 1995, many of the rescue workers needed to learn how to use respirators immediately so they could work in the dusty and asbestos-laden remains of the building. A local 3M OH&ESD team set up shop blocks away from the damaged building to provide respirators and train rescue workers.

Safety-Kleen Corp.

Safety-Kleen is the world's largest recycler of industrial and automotive waste fluids. Its customers are generators of small quantities of waste fluids, such as auto repair shops, auto body shops, dry cleaners, and printers. Safety-Kleen offers customers a "closed-loop" distribution and collection system. This means that from the time Safety-Kleen collects the waste from a customer until it is reclaimed or recovered, it is never managed by another company. In 1994, Safety-Kleen collected and reclaimed more the 230 million gallons of waste fluids.

The forces that stimulated Safety-Kleen to develop a customer education strategy had their beginnings in 1976 when Congress legislated the first federal hazardous waste regulations, RCRA. Congress aimed these regulations at large producers of hazardous wastes. So sweeping were the new regulations that the federal government gave industry four years to prepare for enforcement. In 1980, Congress legislated CERCLA, also known as "Superfund," which mandated the cleanup of hazardous waste sites. In 1984, RCRA was reauthorized as HSWA. This expanded regulation to wastes beyond those listed in RCRA and to small-quantity generators of hazardous wastes. And in 1986, the OSHA legislated the Hazard Communication Standard, also known as the "employee right-to-know" law. It mandated that companies teach their employees about the hazardous wastes used in the workplace.

This mounting federal legislation eventually hit the small waste-producing businesses, and confusion ensued. Most of the federal regulations were written for large generators of hazardous waste, and the small generators were immediately faced with complying with regulations that were not designed for them. The federal regulations also assume that generators, regardless of size, have the technical expertise and management infrastructure to comply with the regulations. Small generators typically do not have this expertise and it is very expensive for them to acquire it.

Safety-Kleen saw the gap between the hazardous waste legislation and small waste producers' knowledge and skills as an opportunity to build stronger relationships with its customers. The aim of Safety-Kleen's customer education strategy is to provide peace of mind to customers by managing their waste fluids, protecting them from liability, protecting their employees, and protecting the environment.

PROGRAMS

In 1988 Safety-Kleen launched its first customer education program, Right-to-Know. A second program, How to Comply with Hazardous Waste Laws, was added in 1990. And a third program, Introduction to Regulatory Compliance, was added in 1994. In addition, Safety-Kleen offers supplemental education in the form of newsletters and updates. There are three variations of the seminars and training materials to address three primary Safety-Kleen customers: vehicle maintenance, printing and graphics, and general industry. The content and context of each of the variations addresses the specific needs of that market segment.

Right-to-Know. The Right-to-Know program has two elements: a train-the-trainer seminar and an employee training seminar. The purpose of the train-the-trainer seminar is to train a few employees in a customer's company how to teach a Right-to-Know course at their company. The course covers both technical knowledge about the right-to-know legislation and knowledge and skills for training fellow employees. The following are key topics in the Right-to-Know seminar:

- Writing a hazard communication program
- Preparing a hazard materials inventory
- How to train employees
- Writing and reading materials safety data sheets (MSDS)
- How to read and inspect container labels

The Right-to-Know course is also taught directly to employees. Customers can hire Safety-Kleen to teach this course on-site or buy training materials from Safety-Kleen so employees who have attended the train-the-trainer seminar can teach the course. The package of training materials includes the following:

- Trainer guide and manual
- Employee training manuals
- MSDS binder with a chemical index system
- Colorful display posters
- Certificates of completion

How to Comply with Hazardous Waste Laws. This seminar, introduced in 1990, teaches customers how to comply with hazardous waste laws. It was a natural seminar for Safety-Kleen to offer customers, because Safety-Kleen had been developing expertise with the laws for years. Topics in the seminar include the following:

- Classifications of hazardous waste
- Obtaining an EPA ID number
- Storing and handling wastes on-site
- Preparing hazardous waste containers for off-site shipments
- Selecting a reliable transporter and waste disposal firm
- Maintaining proper records

- Protecting against real estate property liability
- Understanding EPA inspection and enforcement processes
- Handling on-the-job emergencies
- Other environmental regulations

The seminar materials are shown in Exhibit 7–6:

- Manager resource guide
- Employee training booklets
- Emergency response "Info-Center" chart
- Certificates of completion

Introduction to Regulatory Compliance. Safety-Kleen's third and most recently developed seminar is an overview of compliance regulations from the three federal agencies that enforce hazardous waste legislation:

- OSHA/Workplace Safety
- EPA/Environmental Issues
- DOT/Transportation Safety

The content of the seminar and accompanying materials focus on discussing the regulations from each of these agencies that apply to Safety-Kleen's primary customers: automotive, manufacturing, printing, machine shop, and industrial facilities. Key content in the seminar includes the following:

- Facility analysis
- Documentation required by OSHA, EPA, and DOT
- Training required by OSHA, EPA, and DOT
- Inspections required by OSHA, EPA, and DOT
- Specific state information

Materials for the seminar include a 400-page reference guide, sample forms and worksheets, and certificates of completion.

Newsletters and Updates. To maintain an ongoing educational relationship with customers, Safety-Kleen offers a newsletter and manual updates. The "Total Compliance" newsletter is a monthly forum for communicating compliance information to customers. A typical issue includes a major compliance news story, updates on OSHA and EPA regulations, a case study of how a customer tackled a compliance problem, updates on state regulations, and a question-and-answer column.

Exhibit 7-6   Materials for the Compliance Seminar

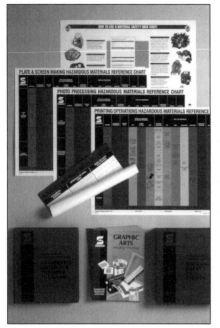

Photographs courtesy of Safety-Kleen Corp.

Updates to the compliance manuals are sent twice a year to customers who attended the Introduction to Regulatory Compliance or How to Comply seminars. These updates ensure that the compliance manuals contain the latest regulatory information.

RESULTS

Safety-Kleen's customer education strategy has delivered the following results:

- 95 percent of participants report that they are more pleased with Safety-Kleen after the seminar than before.
- Customers are more likely to remain a Safety-Kleen customer if they participate in a Safety-Kleen seminar.
- Over 61,000 companies and 155,000 people have participated in Safety-Kleen's customer education programs.
- Nine instructors deliver over 1,000 seminars annually.

Hewlett-Packard

Hewlett-Packard (HP) designs, manufactures, and services electronic products and systems for measurement, computation, and communications. Its basic business purpose is to create information products that accelerate the advancement of knowledge and improve the effectiveness of people and organizations. The company's products and services are used in industry, business, engineering, science, medicine, and education in more than 120 countries.[2]

HP's Computer Systems Organization (CSO) uses customer education as a key element of its selling strategy. The CSO's business focuses on marketing UNIX-based computing systems for multi-user, server-based networks and single-user workstations. It aims to sell customers solutions to their problems, not just computers. As such, an organizational element of CSO is the Professional Services Division (PSD). PSD's mission is to support the sale of HP computing systems by providing consulting, systems integration, and educational services. The customers education need stems from constant technological innovation, requiring specialized knowledge and skills to realize the full potential of the technology. HP educational strategies offer solutions that address all phases of a company's adoption of or transition to state-of-the-art computing environments.

PROGRAMS

HP's customer education strategy is built around providing educational solutions for everyone within the customer's organization. This strategy ensures that everyone who plays a role in selecting, planning, integrating, and using HP products develops the necessary attitude and skills to work successfully with the computing environment.

Business Executives. Executives create business vision, articulate the need for change, and lead the transition process. Providing them with information technology (IT) knowledge enables them to sponsor transitions to new technologies more effectively. The HP customer education programs aimed at business executives typically focus on these topics:

- How to support strategic business objectives in an open client/ server computing environment.

- How the environment will manage the flow of information.
- How to transition the company to new technologies.

HP's executive programs are customized to the needs of the customer and feature presentations by HP and industry experts.

Information Technology Managers. IT managers translate business goals into tangible activities and align business and IT strategies. Their needs for education revolve around understanding new technologies, supporting new technologies, and managing the human resources needed to implement and maintain new technologies. They also need to know how new technologies will affect business strategies and what competitive advantages can be gained from the new technologies. Customer education programs for IT managers typically include these topics:

- Risk management
- Organizational change through technology
- Business process improvement
- Investing in IT

Information Technology Professionals and Users. IT professionals and users lead the implementation of new technologies, use the technology in their day-to-day jobs, and build and manage technology systems. Their needs focus on understanding the technical specifications of the technology, the benefits of the technology, and how technologies work together to meet the needs of the business.

HP directs at this audience a comprehensive system of over 100 courses. HP organizes courses into curriculum paths, a series of courses that address a key topic. Examples of curriculum paths include the following:

- UNIX systems
- Networking
- HP Open View
- UNIX system programming
- Object-oriented technology
- MPE/iX system operation and management

Within these curriculum paths, HP offers customers a variety of course delivery options:

- **Scheduled courses** are public courses offered at HP training sites around the world. They are led by expert HP instructors and offer the opportunity of sharing best practices with fellow participants.
- **Dedicated courses** are similar to scheduled courses except that they are only for employees of a customer's company to ensure confidentiality. Course content is customized to address the customer's needs, and the course can occur at either HP or customer sites.
- **Self-paced courses** are offered in print, on-line, or on video, providing customers educational solutions they can complete at their own pace.
- **Technical satellite seminars** are live broadcasts that cover advanced topics and emerging technologies. HP also offers customers videotapes of these seminars.

HP also offers custom course design services that address the specific needs of customers: needs assessment, curriculum design and development, course delivery, and follow-up and evaluation.

RESULTS

CSO's solutions selling strategy and PSD's educational programs have contributed to making HP number one in the following areas:

- Overall customer satisfaction for the HP 3000
- Overall customer satisfaction for HP-UX (among all UNIX-based operating systems)
- Network and systems management
- Worldwide revenues for UNIX-based computers
- Worldwide X terminal revenues
- Worldwide commercial RISC/UNIX-based computer sales
- Worldwide RISC-based revenues

Summary

This chapter surveyed customer education strategies and programs from five companies. The key items to remember from this chapter include the following:

- Companies develop customer education programs to resolve critical business needs.
- Customer education programs are part of solutions selling strategies.
- Customer education programs target the three types of customers: buyers, users, and resellers.
- Companies use various methods to deliver customer education programs to customers, not just instructor-led courses and user manuals.

Implementing Customer Education Programs

Every customer education program needs an implementation plan that doubles as a marketing strategy. Customer education as a whole is a marketing strategy that fits within the four aspects of marketing: product, price, promotion, and distribution. However, the customer education programs you develop will need their own marketing strategy to assure they are adopted and used by customers. You can have the greatest customer education programs in the world, but if you cannot put them into the hands of customers, they will not deliver the results you expect.

In a marketing framework of product, price, promotion, and distribution, the customer education program is the product. Planning is needed to position the program, price the program, promote the program, and deliver the program. (See Exhibit 8–1.) Positioning relates to how customers perceive the customer education program. The positioning guides how you price your customer education program, whether you offer it for free or sell it for top dollar. Promoting involves announcing to customers that you have customer education programs, stimulating the demand for their use. Distribution is how you put customer education into the hands of customers, including everything from registering

Exhibit 8–1   Elements for Implementing a Customer Education Program

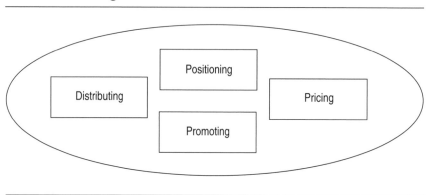

customers for classes to assuring that demonstration products arrive at your training site on time and undamaged.

Positioning

Positioning, a strategy for painting a picture in the customer's mind of what your product is all about, is a critical element of your customer education program.[1] You need to establish in your customer's mind the purpose and value of the customer education you offer. If your product needs some form of instruction to ensure customer success with it, then you will position the instruction as a product feature. If your customers desperately need education in your company's area of expertise, then perhaps positioning your customer education as a stand-alone product will enable you to generate additional revenue. Other kinds of positioning include value-added service and knowledge building. Regardless of which positioning strategy you choose, the way you position your customer education will directly influence the other elements of your implementation plan.

PRODUCT FEATURE POSITIONING

Customer education positioned as a product feature is the most common form of positioning. It means that the instruction sheet, user manual, or instructional video is an integral part of the product. Without it, customers would be wary of buying the product and would most likely fail in their preparation and use of the product. For example, customers would not buy software without a user manual, prepared food without nutritional information or preparation instructions, or prescription medicines without information about indications, doses, and side effects. The message the product feature positioning sends to the customer is that the product includes everything they need to use it successfully. Always position customer education as a product feature if customers cannot prepare or use the product without it, it is required by a regulatory agency, all competing products include it, or customers expect it.

VALUE-ADDED SERVICE POSITIONING

Value-added service is typically an extension of the customer education programs offered as product features. Whereas customer education positioned as a product feature is required by customers, the value-added service positioning relates to learning experiences that are important, but not required. In other words, customers do not expect these experiences but will value them. They include training classes, documentation updates, user bulletins, seminars, access to electronic bulletin boards, and yearly organized events. For example, Home Depot offers home maintenance seminars that are not required to use a product successfully but help customers learn some important tips and tricks to make their projects easier to complete. Position customer education as a value-added service if you want to differentiate the product from the competition, meet needs expressed by a portion of your customers, increase customers' cost of switching to a competing product, or build customer loyalty to the product.

KNOWLEDGE BUILDER POSITIONING

The primary aim of a knowledge builder is to provide customers sufficient information to feel comfortable buying a product. Potential customers commonly fear a sales encounter if they are not familiar with a product. After all, customers do not want to flaunt their lack of knowledge in places like computer stores. An example of this kind of positioning is Gibson Guitar's booklet "How to Buy an Electric Guitar," which gives customers basic information and builds their comfort level for discussing guitar products with salespeople in music stores. What these customers need is a safe environment where they can learn about a product without the risk of embarrassment. Customer education programs positioned as knowledge builders offer this comfort. But knowledge builders can have a secondary aim as well. When companies are trying to sway public opinion after adverse publicity or when proposed legislation could hurt their business, knowledge builders serve to educate customers on the companies' perspective. To fight legislation that would place tobacco products under the jurisdiction of the Food and Drug Administration, R.J. Reynolds offered customers and the public a 12-page brochure and Youth Education Kit on the topic of underage smoking.[2] Position customer education as a knowledge builder if there are high levels of customer anxiety during the sales process, you offer a new class of product not yet experienced by customers, you offer a highly complex and technical product, competitors employ a similar strategy, there are high levels of customer misconceptions due to adverse publicity, or proposed legislation could affect your business.

STAND-ALONE PRODUCT POSITIONING

Customer education positioned as a stand-alone product reflects the company's expertise in a certain discipline. If everyone wants the company's knowledge, it can package the knowledge and sell it to customers as a unique product. Ski instruction and golf lessons are examples of customer education positioned as stand-alone products. In some respects, these forms of customer education are value-added services. Yet customer desire to become proficient in these leisure activities is high enough that they are willing to pay for knowledge.

If the product you sell enables a customer to go into business providing services for or with that product, it is an opportunity for positioning your customer education as a stand-alone product. Macromedia Director, a multimedia authoring program, has enabled thousands of small entrepreneurs to form multimedia production businesses around the product. In this setting, the best developers get the most business. Thus, knowledge and skills are at a premium. Macromedia positions its training classes as stand-alone products separate from its software products and charges top dollar for budding developers to attend.

Position customer education as a stand-alone product under any of the following conditions:

- Customers demand access to your knowledge bases.

- Customers can turn the knowledge of your product into a business.

- Your products deal with leisure activities.

- The educational product will not offend customers in terms of feeling that you are trying to squeeze every last dime from them.

- There is historical precedence in the marketplace for offering stand-alone customer education vehicles.

- Competitors offer similar products and services.

Pricing

Pricing customer education is a challenge for many companies. Customers often expect that customer education will be free. Companies, on the other hand, want to recover the costs associated with developing, distributing, and maintaining customer education programs. To accommodate both, the cost of customer education programs typically get buried in the product's purchase price. Customers never really see the true cost of user manuals, training courses, and other types of programs, reinforcing the belief that they are free.

This perception is changing. More and more business customers see customer education as a means to outsource their internal training and development departments. Rather than developing courses internally, they can often acquire courses from a vendor at a significant savings. In these cases, the need for quality solutions outweighs the need for free solutions. Thus, the perception that customer education must be free is dissipating.

Pricing customer education depends on several factors. How you position your customer education has the greatest impact on price, because positioning sets customer expectations about what they are getting. You also need to consider the limitations, or conditions, you associate with customer education so customers do not get more than they are entitled to. And to ensure customers can always get what they want, always provide the opportunity for customizing customer education.

EFFECTS OF POSITIONING ON PRICING

The way you position your customer education will have an affect on how you price it. (See Exhibit 8–2.) Customers will not pay for customer education that they perceive is a product feature. After all, would you pay an extra $25 for a user manual to accompany a product that cost $150? If the user manual is integral to ensuring one's success with the product, then there should be no additional charge. You will recoup your costs for the user manual by increasing the total price of the product to include the cost of the user manual, plus a profit margin.

You can also expect that customers will not pay for knowledge builders, at least not knowingly. There have been cases where a company will charge for a seminar on a hot topic, such as estate planning, only to turn it into a forum for selling videos, books, and consulting services. Customers will see through this kind of farce, destroying your opportunity to build a long-term relationship with them. Remember that customers do not pay for sales calls, so why should they pay for education that will help them choose your product? If you must charge customers for a knowledge builder, consider repositioning the customer education as a stand-alone product.

Customer education that is considered a value-added service usually has a price associated with it, because the education a company offers will enable customers to reduce their costs of using or operating the product. A simple economic equation drives this type of pricing: the investment in education will provide a significant return.

The price companies change for value-added customer education typically enables them to break even on the service. Customers find this arrangement to be reasonable and fair. The return on investment companies seek through these at-cost programs is to build customer relationships, ensuring that customers will continue to do business with the

Exhibit 8–2   Recommendations for Pricing Customer Education

Position	Price
Product feature	Never
Value-added service	Most of the time
Knowledge builder	Never
Stand-alone product	Always

company over time. By ensuring that customers are completely trained with its own products, a company increases the cost customers must incur if they switch to a competing product. Some companies believe that the value of long-term customers outweighs the cost of providing customer education, so they offer value-added customer education programs for free.

If customers discover that the company intends to turn a profit on its value-added customer education programs, the company loses its opportunity for building a relationship with the customer. Customers might come to believe that the company is intentionally building complexity into a product to stimulate demand for training.

Of course, there is always a price for customer education that is a stand-alone product. And in true capitalist form, the price charged should be what the market will bear. The objective is to make money from the knowledge you possess, because you obviously spent significant resources acquiring that knowledge.

LIMITING CUSTOMER EDUCATION EXPOSURE

Regardless of how you price your customer education, you must establish reasonable limitations to ensure that you can accurately budget the cost of the programs and limit unreasonable customer demands.

For self-instructional programs that accompany a product, it is perfectly reasonable to charge customers for new materials when the original materials have been lost or damaged. Some companies charge full price, others charge only shipping and handling, and others offer it for free. Ruger, a manufacturer of guns, engraves a statement on the barrel of its Mark II .22 pistol offering a free instructional manual to anyone who writes to request one. The offer here reflects Ruger's commitment to customer safety and satisfaction with an inherently dangerous   product.

For classroom or one-on-one educational programs, the common limitations are frequency, duration, attendance, location, and amenities. (See Exhibit 8–3.) Frequency relates to how often you offer the customer education. Do you provide it before product installation, during product installation, at specific intervals after product installation, or all of the above? Duration relates to the length of the program. Do you measure it in hours, days, or weeks? Attendance relates to the minimum or maximum number of learners who will attend the program. If you have designed and priced your program for 20 people, it will not be cost-effective if only three register. Location relates to where you will

Exhibit 8–3   Common Limitations for Classroom and One-on-One Educational Programs

Limitation	Description	Example
Frequency	The number of times you offer a customer education program	We will hold the educational program once, one week before product installation.
Duration	The length of the customer education program	The educational program is one day.
Attendance	The minimum or maximum number of learners	The maximum number of participants for the educational program is six.
Location	Where the customer education program is held	We will hold the education program at the customer's site in conference room 6B.
Amenities	The "extras" provided during the educational program	We will provide lunch for all participants.

conduct the program: at the customer's site, at a hotel or conference center, or at your offices or training center. Amenities are the "extras" you offer during the program: a meal, refreshments, or writing materials with your company's logo imprinted on them.

CUSTOMIZATION

Limitations are necessary to control costs associated with providing customer education, but they do not prevent you from customizing your education to meet specific customers' needs.

You should know your customers well enough to make simple adjustments within educational programs without incurring additional costs. A common request is to make examples and problems within the course relate to their business. For example, teaching people in an advertising agency how to use a new phototypesetter will likely be different from teaching people in a book publishing company. The focus of the advertising agency reflects the need to create a wide variety of typographic treatments for short blocks of text. The focus of the book publisher, on the other hand, reflects the need for handling vast amounts of text in a relatively standardized form. Teaching the book publisher how to use the phototypesetter through examples that relate to advertising is not an effective means of instruction.

For customization requests that go beyond replacing examples, you should pass your costs for performing the customization to the customer. For example, if you price your educational programs based on conducting the program at the customer's site, but the customer prefers an off-site location, then you will pass those costs along to the customer. If the customer wants major modifications for your educational programs to reflect not only business needs, but also company culture, consistency with other training programs, and special materials, then by all means charge them for the service. Some companies charge customers an hourly rate, and others charge a fixed price. Some negotiate customization to be included in the total purchase price of the product the customer is buying. If this is the case, be sure you describe the nature of the customization precisely in the terms and conditions of sale to limit your exposure to excessive costs.

SETTING THE PRICE

Pricing anything, whether a product, an educational program, or customization, is an intricate science, the scope of which cannot be fully explored in this book. However, one basic pricing model, a break-even analysis, can help you calculate the minimum price you need to collect from customers to recoup the costs of providing the customer education. The primary elements of a break-even analysis are volume, fixed costs, and variable costs. Volume is the number of user manuals you will ship or the number of courses you will conduct. Fixed costs relate to the cost of developing the educational program, such as the cost of writing and designing a user manual or an instructor-led course, or the overhead associated with maintaining an educational program, such as the cost of an administrator who registers customers for classes. These costs are fixed because they are incurred once or do not vary depending on volume. Variable costs relate to the cost of reproducing each user manual or holding a course. These costs will vary depending on the total number of manuals produced or the number of courses you run. The formula for finding the break-even price follows:

$$\text{Break-even price per unit} = \frac{\text{Fixed costs} + (\text{Volume} \times \text{Variable costs})}{\text{Volume}}$$

Exhibit 8–4 shows a break-even analysis for a user manual. The fixed costs associated with developing a user manual are $33,500. The variable costs are $4.82. If the company expects to ship 1,000 products, then it must build into its cost of goods sold (CGS) $38.32 for each manual just to recoup its costs. A user manual is typically considered a component of the whole product, so the price per manual becomes a component of the CGS. The CGS reflects all the variable costs that go into producing a marketable product. The CGS is also the point at which companies determine the markup, or margin, that contributes to setting the price customers will ultimately pay.

Exhibit 8–5 shows a similar break-even analysis for an instructor-led course. Here, the fixed costs include both the cost of developing the

Exhibit 8–4 Data for a Break-Even Analysis of a User Manual

Fixed Costs		
Technical writing	$20,000	
Graphic design	10,000	
Camera-ready art	3,500	
Total fixed costs		$33,500
Variable Costs		
Printing	$4.50	
Packaging	.32	
	$4.82	
Total variable costs		$4,820
Total costs		$38,320
Break-Even		
Volume (Number of manuals)	1,000	
Price per manual		$38.32

$$\$38.32 \;=\; \frac{\$33,500 + (1,000 \times \$4.82)}{1,000}$$

course and the cost of administering the course, such as registering students, organizing materials, and handling logistics. Variable costs include the cost of the instructor, instructor travel, a site for the course (a hotel meeting room and associated equipment), and the materials for ten students. (In the case of this course, the number of students per class is another variable expense you need to consider. We have assumed an average of ten students per class.) If the number of classes the company expects to conduct is 100, then the company must recoup $4,050 for each course, or $405 for each student.

Exhibit 8–5   Data for a Break-Even Analysis of an Instructor-Led Course

Fixed Costs		
Course development	$50,000	
Course administration	20,000	
Total fixed costs		$ 70,000
Variable Costs		
Instructor	$ 600.00	
Travel	950.00	
Site	1,500.00	
Materials (10 students)	300.00	————
	$3,350.00	
Total variable costs		$335,000
Total costs		$405,000
Break-Even		
Volume (Number of classes)	100	
Price per class		$4,050
Price per student		$405

$$4{,}050 = \frac{\$70{,}000 + (100 \times \$4{,}450)}{100}$$

Pricing for customer education positioned as a stand-alone product uses the break-even formulas described above but adds a variable called the profit margin. Profit margin is the difference between your costs and the selling price you charge customers. For example, the cost of the user manual in Exhibit 8–4 was $38.32. To earn a 30 percent profit margin from sales of the user manual, you would charge customers $54.74 for each manual, using the following formula:

$$\$54.57 \ = \ \frac{\$\,38.32}{(1-.30)}$$

The tricky part of all of these analyses is forecasting the volume accurately. If the volume you predict is too high, then you experience a loss. If the volume you predict is too low, then you experience a gain (and for some positioning strategies, the price you are charging is too high). Exhibit 8–6 illustrates the effects of poor forecasting. You can increase the accuracy of your predictions by knowing the size of your market, historical sales volume, projected increase in market size, planned marketing activities that will stimulate demand in the existing markets or open new markets, and the activities of your competition.

An important lesson learned from the pricing of customer education is that the price you charge often reflects the value customers place on the education. If you offer the education for free, customers may not place high value on it. Customers will skip classes and avoid reading the manuals. Charging for customer education elevates its importance in the mind of the customer, creating the perception that the education has value and is worthwhile. It also ensures that customers respect the educational commitment and fully participate in educational programs.

Promoting

An educational program without an audience is worthless. Without an audience, you cannot achieve the objectives you set. Promoting your customer education programs ensures that customers know programs exist and helps stimulate demand. Promotion can be as simple as listing a user manual on a sales sheet's feature/benefit table, or as complex as producing a program guide. Promotion involves such activities as advertising, personal selling, sales promotion, publicity, and collateral

Exhibit 8-6   Effects of Inaccurate Predictions

Prediction Too High

Predicted volume	1,000	
Actual volume	437 @ $38.32	**$16,745.84**
Fixed costs		$33,500.00
Variable costs	437 @ $4.82	2,106.34
Total costs		**$35,606.34**
Gain (Loss)		($18,860.50)

Prediction Too Low

Predicted volume	1,000	
Actual volume	1,856 @ $38.32	**$71,121.92**
Fixed costs		$33,500.00
Variable costs	1,856 @ $4.82	8,945.92
Total costs		**$42,445.92**
Gain (Loss)		$28,676.00

materials. The mix of activities you select to promote your programs will relate to the positioning of your programs.

ADVERTISING CUSTOMER EDUCATION PROGRAMS

One common use of advertising in customer education is to promote the availability of knowledge builders. Every year, hundreds of advertisements will offer booklets, brochures, seminars, and videotapes that provide customers the up-front knowledge and skills they need to make decisions about buying products or supporting a company's political agenda. Gibson Guitar's print ads offer a "How to Buy an Electric Guitar" booklet. NordicTrack's mix of television and print ads offer both booklets and videotapes. R.J. Reynolds' print ads offer brochures and Youth Education Kits. And First American Discount Corporation's television ads offer free copies of investment dictionaries. In many cases, customer responses to these offers are then used as entry points for follow-up calls by sales representatives or for collecting public opinion data.

Customer education positioned as a product feature has always been a staple element of product advertisements. The basic messages communicated in these ads are *declarative* (we have a training program for customers) or *comparative* (our manuals are better than the competition's manuals). Apple Computer used comparative advertising for many years in promoting the Macintosh. Ads featured a stack of user manuals for a competing computer, compared to the few slim manuals for the Macintosh. The message was clear: our products are so simple to use that you do not need lots of user manuals to become proficient.

Ads that promote customer education's position as a value-added service or stand-alone product can either tout the education as an incentive for buying the product it supports or stimulate the demand for the service or educational product. Microsoft used the first strategy in a flight of ads for Microsoft Office.[3] The ad offers customers who buy any Microsoft Office product a free interactive training tool valued at $79.95, or a $50 rebate if the customer attends any Microsoft-approved training class.

As an example of the second strategy, IBM's ad campaign for its HelpWare™ program of support and educational services emphasized the existence of the HelpWare program and communicated the features and benefits of the program components. It did not attempt to sell IBM computers. Similarly, Macromedia's direct-mail campaign for its line of Director software courses did not address buying the Director product. Rather, its purpose was to stimulate existing Director owners to register for Director classes.

PERSONAL SELLING OF CUSTOMER EDUCATION PROGRAMS

The sales and customer service functions of your organization provide personal sales opportunities for your customer education programs. Employees can personally invite customers to seminars, explain specific educational features of the product, and stimulate demand for educational programs that are value-added services and stand-alone products. Safety-Kleen has found that its existing sales and customer service infrastructure is the only cost-effective means it has to promote its educational programs. With a customer base of over 500,000, direct mail is much too complex and expensive. The sales and service force, on the other hand, has week-to-week contact with all customers, providing the vehicle to distribute educational program literature and personally invite customers to the programs.

As more and more companies embrace a solutions selling strategy for marketing their products, the need for your sales force to inform customers about educational programs will continue to rise. Using techniques suited for educating customers, sales and customer service training programs need to develop people's ability to recognize customer education opportunities and explain product features and benefits. Incentive programs need to include measures that relate to relationship-building activities with customers, such as their attendance at customer education programs.

SALES PROMOTION FOR CUSTOMER EDUCATION

The aim for sales promotion related to customer education is to provide opportunities for customers to try the educational program before they fully commit to attending the program or buying the product the product supports. Allowing customers to sample the educational programs is very important. Shoppers in grocery stores will often read instructions on the side of cake mixes to check how easy it is to bake the cake. However, many products do not permit customers access to instruction manuals and user guides prior to the sale. If your product falls into this trap, consider enabling retailers or sales reps to show customers those manuals during the sales process.

Sampling is also important for programs positioned as value-added services and stand-alone products. You should invite decision makers (or their representatives) to attend your educational programs for free as a means for them to evaluate the program's format and content. Their decision (or recommendation) could cause several hundred people from their company to sign up for your programs. As with any sampling activity, be sure someone from your organization debriefs the customer after the program. This allows you to gauge their interest in the program and provides opportunities to upsell them on customization of the programs.

Knowledge builders are best served by such promotional tactics as coupons. There is no harm in setting a price for your pre-sales knowledge building programs, then offering everyone you meet a free coupon to attend your seminar or to receive your booklet. You will stimulate demand for your programs and increase the perceived value of the content.

PUBLICITY FOR CUSTOMER EDUCATION

Publicity for your customer education program can be as simple as an announcement in the community activities section of your local newspaper or as sophisticated as a feature article in an industry trade journal describing a success story attributed to your educational programs. Publicity can also cross over into internal employee newsletters, providing recognition for employees who successfully complete your educational programs. Also, recognize that more and more product reviews in journals and magazines will include an assessment of the quality of your educational programs. Be sure your press kits point out the features and benefits of your educational programs. It can contribute to better differentiating your products from the competition. Here are some common events associated with customer education that call for publicity:

- Total number of people trained through your programs (the 100,000 attendance mark or a similar milestone is definitely worth announcing.)
- Recognition of the first class to complete your educational programs (typically used in internal customer newsletters)
- Measurable reduction in accidents, failures, or breakdowns attributed to your educational programs
- Measurable improvement in production, sales, or quality attributed to your educational programs
- Announcements of new educational programs offered to customers
- Announcements of scheduled, public educational programs
- Awards your educational programs have won

COLLATERAL MATERIALS FOR CUSTOMER EDUCATION

To support the primary forms of promotion described above, any promotional campaign needs collateral materials that detail the elements of a customer education program. Collateral materials are typically needed only for programs positioned as value-added services and stand-alone products. For individual programs, the primary collateral piece is a program description. For a series of programs, the primary collateral piece is a program catalog.

Program Description. A program description most closely equates with a college course syllabus. It is typically in the form of a single sales sheet, but it can also be several pages or organized into a small brochure. The program description should include the following elements:

- **Program overview.** A one- to two-paragraph description of the educational program will typically summarize the customer's need (or business need) and the goals of the program.
- **Audience.** This plainly states who should and who should not attend, subscribe, or order the educational program. For example, salespeople should not attend a program designed for product engineers. If your program has any prerequisites or required qualifications, you should list them as well.
- **Key objectives.** These are statements describing what the learner will be able to do upon completing the course. The generally accepted format of these statements is an action verb followed by a description of the desired behavior. Avoid imprecise action verbs such as "understand" and "learn" in your statements, because it is difficult to measure the behaviors associated with these words. Instead, use an action verb that is measurable or observable. (See Exhibit 8–7.)
- **Course structure and content.** This is an outline of the course, describing each of the major sections and the content that will be covered in each section. The intention is to give learners a better sense of how the educational program will enable them to accomplish the objectives. If necessary, the structure should also include timing for the various sections. Exhibit 8–8 shows an example of a course structure statement.

Exhibit 8–7　Key Objectives

Upon completing this course, you will be able to:

- List the three products in the product line.
- Describe the features and benefits of each product.
- Assemble each product.
- Lead a class that teaches other employees how to assemble the products.

Exhibit 8–8   Course Structure Statement

Day 1

8:30≠a.m.	Course Overview and Participant Introduction
8:30–10:00 A.M.	Three Models of the X500
	• X500 Classic
	• X500 E
	• X500 Turbo
10:00–10:15 A.M.	Break
10:15–12 noon	Assembling the X500 Classic
	• Inventorying product parts
	• Tools required for assembly
	• Assembly procedures
	• Quality control and testing
12 noon–1 P.M.	Lunch (Served in the cafeteria)

- **Learning methods and facilities.** Customers like to know about the methods you use to teach your courses and the facilities required for the course. The following are common questions about methods:

  - Are classes lecture-based, problem-based, or case-based?
  - How much time is spent in lecture versus the time spent hands-on with the product?
  - Does your self-instructional video program have an accompanying guidebook?
  - Is there a certification test embedded in your computer-based training program?

  Facilities can describe your own training facilities or the facility needs required at a customer's site or off-site location.

- **Instructor biography.** The value all learners place on educational programs depends on who is behind the program. Linking the content to an industry organization or a well-known expert promotes its value. Fleet Finance used this tactic in descriptions of its courses and booklets by linking the National Consumers League as a partner in their development.

- **Schedule, options, and terms and conditions.** This is the "business" part of the course description. If your programs are offered on a schedule, then you need to list the schedule, preferably for the coming year. Also describe any options available for the program, such as customization, on-site delivery, or licensing. Terms and conditions should address pricing, payment policies, maximum number of learners for a class, cancellation policies, and other limitations associated with the program.
- **Response mechanism.** Always be sure to include a means for customers to respond to the offer contained within the course description—attending or ordering the course. A telephone number is the preferred mechanism, but you should also include a registration form that the customer can mail or fax, an e-mail address, or a World Wide Web address.

Program Catalog. In its simplest form, a program catalog gathers a series of program descriptions and assembles them in a central resource, or catalog. However, if you offer enough programs to warrant a program catalog (three or more is a good rule of thumb), you might want to consider adding features to make it easier for customers to decide which programs are best for them. An example of a program catalog is shown in Exhibit 8–9. One feature of many catalogs is a program map: a pathway that shows customers the sequence of courses they should take to become proficient in a certain topic. In Hewlett-Packard's customer education catalog, there are several program maps (they call them curriculum maps) for various topic areas, such as UNIX and networking. (See Exhibit 8–10.)

Another feature of a program catalog is the grouping of terms and conditions and response mechanisms in one section, rather than localized to each specific program. Of course, if you offer an 800-number registration line, be sure to include that number on each page of your catalog. Learning facilities can also be grouped under its own section. In both the Hewlett-Packard and Tandem Computers customer education catalogs, descriptions of various training sites and maps showing the location of those sites are presented in a special training site section.

Delivering

If you have ever delivered an educational program you know that anything that can go wrong will go wrong. All trainers have their war

Exhibit 8–9   Customer Education Program Catalog

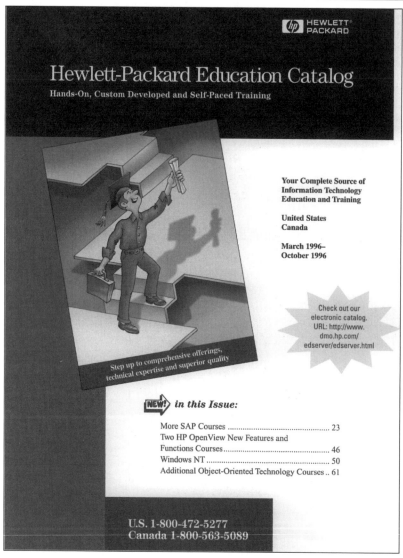

stories. While conducting classes in Poland and Hungary, the author learned that central heating systems in those countries are usually not turned on unless the temperature drops below 18°C for three days in a row. As luck would have it, classes always began on the first day of such a cold spell and ended on the third. Learning (or teaching) in a

Exhibit 8-10 A Program Map for a Series of HP Courses

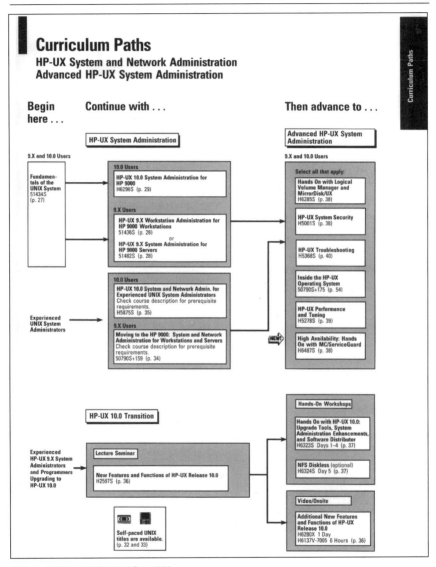

© Copyright Hewlett-Packard Co., 1996.

refrigerator is next to impossible—you spend most of your time and attention figuring out ways to stay warm. Most U.S. trainers will never face this type of problem, but there are other common mistakes and pitfalls associated with delivering educational programs. The rest of this chapter presents strategies for managing program delivery.

FULFILLMENT SYSTEMS

Before you announce your first educational programs to your customers, make sure you have systems in place to manage fulfillment: handling incoming requests from customers, processing those requests, and delivering programs to satisfy them. Incoming calls, mail, faxes, and e-mail from customers who seek information about programs, want to register for programs, or need to order programs should be managed by a trained telemarketer or administrator. This might be through your own department, using an administrative assistant or dedicated program registrar to handle the requests, through the sales department's inbound telemarketing staff, or through the customer service telemarketing staff. To handle a high volume of calls over a limited time, you can also outsource your telemarketing to a qualified vendor. Regardless of who manages inbound calls, be sure to provide these people sufficient information and training about your programs so they can respond effectively to customer questions and requests.

Database systems can and should be set up to manage the information associated with delivering educational programs. To help telemarketers answer common customer questions, the database must allow telemarketers to access program descriptions, schedules, and related information. If the database cannot deliver this information, be sure that telemarketers have this information at their desks. If your programs allow a maximum number of participants per class, the database should prevent telemarketers from scheduling customers for those classes and instead refer to other open dates. The data in the database should be sufficient to generate shipping labels and packing lists for self-instructional materials, confirmation and reminder letters for courses, and participant lists for trainers. If your programs involve certifying or testing participants, the database should have some method of keeping track of participant scores. If you charge for educational programs, your database might also have to tie in with your company's ordering and accounting systems.

You will also need to establish a warehousing and inventory system for distributing self-instructional and classroom materials to both customers and trainers. Depending on the number of programs you offer and the number of customers you serve, your warehousing facilities can be as small as a cabinet in your office or as large as several racks in the central warehouse. Each program you develop should have a unique identification number, or product number, that can be specific to your department or part of the company's central product numbering scheme. The numbering system you choose should have the capability to handle updates and revisions to the original program. To ensure error-free inventory control, consider identifying your programs with bar codes and managing inventory levels in a database system. Both will give you tight control of your inventories and help plan reprinting schedules.

TRAINERS AND INSTRUCTORS

If your educational programs are primarily instructor-led, then you will need to develop and manage a staff of trainers and instructors. There are two schools of thought on recruiting and hiring trainers for customer education programs:

1. Recruit people from within the organization who are technical experts with your products and services and teach them to be trainers.
2. Recruit people who are excellent presenters and trainers and teach them your products.

Both methods have advantages, depending on the structure of your courses. If your courses are primarily hands-on laboratories and complex problem-solving sessions with technical products, you will need experts to lead the class. On the other hand, if you have well-scripted, content-heavy courses, then qualified presenters are preferred. Safety-Kleen hires people who are good presenters mainly because their courses on environmental law and regulations are tightly scripted and the content is factual in nature. The same is true with most of 3M's respirator courses, which are presented by sales representatives. On the other hand, Hewlett-Packard's courses on UNIX programming require an instructor who is first an expert with UNIX, and second a good instructor.

There are two key principles of managing your training staff. One principle is that of redundancy. Having one expert who is a wonderful trainer as your sole source is a dangerous position. Sickness, injury, death, retirement, resignation, or job switching can put you in the unenviable position of having 20 courses scheduled for the next six months and no one who is capable of delivering those courses. Just as public school systems have substitute teachers, you need to make sure you have substitute trainers. Recruit these individuals from within your organization, or look to retirees whom you can call from time to time.

Be sure to provide opportunities for these substitutes to teach or team-teach the courses so they can maintain their skills.

The second principle, related to redundancy, is to require instructors to work from an appropriate leader's guide. A leader's guide is a document that serves as a script for the course. Some leader's guides are simply outlines, and others are detailed scripts. A leader's guide ensures consistency between instructors and serves as an official document for the class, ensuring compliance with legal requirements and establishing a paper trail for product liability defense. Without such controls, instructors might wander, missing key content that could expose customers to problems and dangers. It also ensures that instructors who are experts have documented the knowledge in their head so that the company does not lose that expert's "intellectual property" if he or she leaves the company. The development of a leader's guide should be facilitated by an instructional designer and reviewed by legal counsel.

TRAVEL

A big burden for a customer education organization is travel, in terms of both the stress on trainers and the expense. For example, Safety-Kleen's cadre of nine trainers delivers 1,000 sessions per year. Delivering more than 100 sessions per year chews up 70–80 percent of a person's time. It is no wonder that Safety-Kleen's trainers turn over every three years, as burn out and redundancy wear them down. Safety-Kleen reduces its travel expenses by strategically locating its trainers throughout the country. This ensures that a trainer can reach a customer's site via a short drive or plane trip. Most trainers work from their homes, reducing yet another expense, office space.

SITE LOGISTICS

A complex delivery issue for any type of educational program is the site logistics. Many companies try to avoid logistical problems by holding educational programs at their own dedicated sites. This ensures some semblance of reliability and redundancy with both hands-on demo products and instructional media, such as video players, overhead projectors, and computer presentation systems. It also gives trainers sufficient time to set up the learning environment to meet the needs of the course. The downside, of course, is that customers need to travel to your location, which might be cost-prohibitive.

Design of learning sites should match your instructional methods. For example, if your methods involve team-based learning and group work, a classroom that has chairs and tables bolted to the floor will discourage collaborative activities. A mix of round and square tables with chairs that can be rearranged in the classroom would work better. If your programs involve hands-on activities with equipment, you need to be aware of learner-to-equipment ratios (smaller is better), access to equipment, and the ability of instructors to effectively mentor and coach learners.

Site problems start creeping up as you move from the safety and comfort of a dedicated site to the confusion and uncertainty of off-site locations. Your opportunity to plan ahead is diminished, and you find yourself relying on people you have never met to ensure that your event takes place seamlessly. Hotels change rooms on you at the last minute. Boxes containing all of your class materials, of course, get delivered to the wrong room. Audiovisual specialists arrive late. You expect ten phone lines for practice exercises for 20 people, but you find only two were installed. Your trainer mismarks the date in his or her calendar and fails to show up. These are only a few of the common pitfalls.

Many of these problems do not spell disaster for your program, but they do impact the overall quality and professionalism you are trying to promote, especially to your customers. The best plan is always to expect the worst and have some backup plans to avoid a complete catastrophe:

- When working with hotels, conference centers, and even your own facilities staff, clearly describe your site requirements in writing, preferably using a checklist. For special arrangements of chairs, tables, and equipment, draw a picture.

- Verify all your plans, equipment, and materials a week before delivering the program, and then double-check them the day before.

- If you are displaying your visual aids through a computer and LCD projection unit, bring a set of overhead transparencies just in case the technology does not work or your computer crashes.

- Carry one unbound copy of course materials. If your duplicated materials do not make it to the session, you can usually find a photocopier to make more copies.

- Always make sure there is a flip chart, white board, or chalkboard in the classroom, even if you don't plan to use it. It serves as a handy backup in case all of your visual aids fail. Remember to carry your own pens or chalk, check that pens have sufficient ink, and ensure that erasers are available.

BACK-END SERVICES

Back-end services are everything that occurs after you have delivered the program. Unused materials need to be checked for damage and re-entered into inventory, equipment that broke needs to be repaired, classrooms need to be cleaned and restored to their original state, and materials need to be updated or refined based on suggestions from the learners. If your educational programs involve testing and certifying learners, you will need to establish methods to process tests, record scores, and report results. If the number of learners who attend your programs is low, you can score these tests by hand and record the results in a database. If you have a high volume of learners, then you might consider a Scantron system that automatically reads answers on "bubble sheets" or develop a computer-based testing system.

Summary

Implementing an educational program successfully is a multifaceted process, requiring attention to detail every step of the way. The key-points you should take away from this chapter are as follows:

- Consider your educational program a product with a marketing plan that specifies how you will position, price, promote, and deliver the program.
- Positioning establishes the purpose and value of your educational program in the mind of the customer. The four categories of positioning customer education are product feature, value-added service, knowledge builder, and stand-alone product.
- Pricing depends on positioning. Educational programs positioned as either knowledge builders or product features never have a price to customers. Value-added service programs might or might not have a price. Stand-alone products always have a price.
- Promotion focuses on how you will announce the educational program to customers and encourage them to subscribe. The five forms of promoting customer education are advertising, personal selling, sales promotion, publicity, and marketing collateral.

- Delivery relates to how you will put the educational programs in the hands of customers. You need to consider such issues as fulfillment, hiring and managing staff, scheduling travel, designing and securing training sites, and managing back-end services.

Evaluating Customer Education Programs

How good a basketball player would you be if you never knew whether or not your jump shot ever went into the basket? How long would you keep fishing if you never saw the size of the fish you caught? And would you keep investing money if you never knew how your stocks were performing? Answers: terrible, not very long, and no way. Any action we take as human beings requires some form of feedback to help us learn from our experiences and improve our future performance.

The same principle holds true for customer education. If you never evaluate a program's outcomes, you will never know whether it achieved its aims. Furthermore, you will never improve future customer education programs unless you know what worked and what did not work in existing programs.

Evaluation is the last phase in the instructional systems design model. It is the phase where you link what your program delivers back to the needs that prompted you to develop the program in the first place. For example, if the need you identified was to reduce customer errors, then the solution you developed should measurably contribute to error reduction. If not, you can consider your program both a failure and a valuable learning experience. For what you learn from failure will ultimately make you a better designer of customer education programs.

The focus of this chapter is summative evaluation—the evaluation that occurs after you implement the program. Summative evaluation contrasts with formative evaluation, which occurs during the development of the customer education program. Robert Stake, a leading authority on educational evaluation theory, differentiates formative and summative evaluation using this handy reminder:

Formative evaluation is when the cook tastes the soup . . .
Summative evaluation is when the guests taste the soup.[1]

Proper evaluation is similar to a detective building a case against a suspect, like in the board game Clue. The detective/evaluator first systematically gathers evidence about the case/outcomes. Next, the detective/evaluator analyzes the evidence to determine which evidence is worthwhile in order to draw conclusions about who is guilty/the results of the program: Colonel Mustard did it in the study with the candlestick/the program reduced customer errors. (See Exhibit 9–1.)

Every customer education program must be evaluated in some way. Without evaluation, you have no clue as to the worth of your solution. Evaluation carries significant political and performance implications, the scope of which far exceeds one chapter. Thus, this chapter will focus on the major principles of evaluation and their linkage to customer education programs.

There are three outcomes for any educational program: effectiveness, efficiency, and appeal.

- *Effective* means that the educational program did what it was intended to do: it helped people learn knowledge, skills, or attitudes to resolve a problem.

Exhibit 9–1   The Process of Evaluation

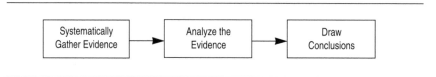

Source: R.M. Gagné, L.J. Briggs, and W.W. Wager. *Principles of Instructional Design.* 4th ed. New York: Harcourt Brace Jovanovich, 1992.

- *Efficient* means that the educational program was cost-effective in terms of the cost to develop, the cost to implement, and the time required to complete the program.

- *Appealing* means that both teachers and students enjoyed the educational program.

Don Kirkpatrick of the University of Wisconsin extended these three basic outcomes to better serve the needs of business. He proposes four levels of evaluation:[2]

- **Reactions:** How well learners liked the education program.

- **Learning:** What knowledge, skills, and attitudes learners acquired.

- **Behavior:** The ability of the learner to use knowledge, skills, and attitudes on the job.

- **Results:** Improved profits, reduced costs, and other similar results.

Evaluating Reactions

The first level of evaluation relates to the satisfaction customers receive from your programs. This is affectionately referred to as the "smiles test." Satisfaction is a valuable measure for customer education programs. It gives you a broad gauge of the quality of the program. If the quality is high, then customers are likely to encourage their peers to complete the program. There is also a strong correlation between a customer liking a program and its impact on the customer's performance.

Questionnaires, interviews with customers, observations or assessments of programs by trained evaluators, and customer letters and comments are the means for collecting evidence about program satisfaction. Exhibit 9–2 shows a portion of Borland Software's questionnaire to assess product documentation. Similar questionnaires are used at the end of an instructor-led course to rate the quality of the course. The questions usually focus on these aspects of the course:

- Quality of the course
- Quality of the instructor
- Relevance of the content to the customer's needs

Exhibit 9–2 Borland's Product Documentation Questionnaire

As you look at the following statements, think about the Borland Languages documentation (including Help) that you've used, and then circle the reponse that reflects your experience.

1 Never, 2 Seldom, 3 Occasionally, 4 Usually, or 5 Always.

1 2 3 4 5 The examples are relevant to how I use the product.

1 2 3 4 5 Examples exist for both basic and complex aspects of the task or feature.

1 2 3 4 5 All examples work as explained.

1 2 3 4 5 There are enough examples.

1 2 3 4 5 The information in the manuals and Help is technically correct.

1 2 3 4 5 The tasks described are the ones I perform.

1 2 3 4 5 When I want more information, I know where to look for it, and I find what I'm looking for.

1 2 3 4 5 The structure of the Help system makes it easy to find information.

1 2 3 4 5 Technical information is sufficiently detailed.

1 2 3 4 5 There is the right amount of overview information.

1 2 3 4 5 There is the right amount of entry-level information.

1 2 3 4 5 There is the right amount of advanced information.

1 2 3 4 5 There is the right amount of problem-solving/troubleshooting information.

1 2 3 4 5 There is enough information to help me do my job.

1 2 3 4 5 The pace of the writing is appropriate (neither too slow or too fast)

1 2 3 4 5 Most of the information in the manuals is necessary.

1 2 3 4 5 Reference documentation is as complete as I need it to be.

1 2 3 4 5 The documentation is written to my level.

1 2 3 4 5 The page layout makes the documentation easy to read.

1 2 3 4 5 Important information stands out.

1 2 3 4 5 I can find the information I require in a reasonable amount of time.

1 2 3 4 5 Manual titles help me go to the book with the right information.

1 2 3 4 5 I don't have to jump around too much to get information.

1 2 3 4 5 The index is complete. I can find the entry I need easily.

1 2 3 4 5 The amount of information I must learn to complete a task is reasonable.

1 2 3 4 5 When I call Borland Technical Support, the support engineer refers me to the product documentation.

Additional Comments:

Developers Conference 3

- Timeliness of the content
- Learning methods and activities

Although questionnaires are efficient and confidential means of data collection, interviews with customers can often gather more specific information about your programs. It is good practice to supplement your questionnaire data with interviews to help further understand customer opinions and attitudes.

Trained evaluators who participate in your classes from time to time and who review your other instructional materials, such as documents, videos, and computer programs, provide an additional level of insight to the quality of your programs. These evaluators can compare the quality of your programs to generally accepted methods and best practices. This is especially helpful if your educational programs are a competitive advantage and you want to maintain the advantage you have over your competitors.

Remember, if customers are truly impressed with your programs, they will tell you about it. Letters from customers praising the worth of your programs or offhand comments when they call to register for another course are additional sources of data that reflect their satisfaction with your programs. All customer education programs should have some form of reaction evaluation.

Evaluating Learning

Evaluating what a customer learns from an educational program is best handled through a test. Multiple-choice tests, fill-in-the-blank tests, essay tests, performance tests (such as a driving test), and oral examinations can be used to assess knowledge and skills in a controlled environment before learners try their new knowledge in the real world. In essence, tests are predictors of success.

CRITERION-REFERENCED TESTING

The kind of test best suited for customer education is called a *criterion-referenced test,* also known as an *objectives test.* The foundation of any instructional program is its goals and objectives. The program designer will define key objectives—what the learner will be able to do after instruction—and enabling objectives—what the learner needs to know to accomplish the key objective. Criterion-referenced tests use the key and enabling objectives as the criteria for the evaluation. For example, if a key objective is "to use a food processor safely," and an enabling objective is "to identify the parts of the food processor," then one item for the test is to make sure the customer can identify the parts of the food processor.

Criterion-referenced tests focus on mastery. You want customers to pass the test and to be successful. However, you need to establish the level of mastery. Ideally, mastery is that customers can correctly answer 100 percent of the questions. Yet will their ultimate performance be effective if they miss identifying one part of the food processor out of the possible ten parts? If performance will not be significantly influenced, then you may adjust your mastery scale to 90 percent, 80 percent, or even 70 percent—the mastery level used for driving tests. In this case, this indicates that you will still be a reasonably safe driver if you pass 70 percent or more of the test questions.

Criterion-referenced tests contrast with norm-referenced tests, which rank the ability of the learners. The Scholastic Aptitude Test (SAT) is an example, as are most of the tests given in schools. These tests distribute learners across a standard distribution, such as a bell curve. In this model, some learners will fail, some learners will earn A's, and most learners will cluster themselves among D's, C's, and B's.

Norm-referenced testing is incompatible with customer education. Your aim should be to ensure that all customers are able to receive A's on the tests you give them. If a customer fails your course, it should be because he or she did not achieve the objectives, never because you are only able to pass a certain number of learners. All customer education tests must be criterion-referenced and focus on some level of mastery.

CERTIFICATION

Some companies need to place an additional level of formality on their customer education programs through a process of certification. Certification is essentially a formal promise that the people who attend your training courses and pass the tests will perform to a certain standard. Certification is very important for educational programs that support high-risk products or performance. For example, an emergency medical technician (EMT) must be certified to operate a defibrillator, a medical device that helps restart a person's heart by sending electricity through a person's body. The danger and risk in not having the EMT certified is high. Thus, the educational program must ensure that graduates have the proper skills through proper testing procedures.

Certification has also become popular in the information technology industry. Microsoft reports that it experienced a tenfold increase in customers it certified through its various training programs. Research by Dataquest indicates that certified professionals deliver value to a business in the following way:

- Providing higher levels of service
- Completing tasks quicker
- Understanding new technologies faster
- Providing leadership to other staff
- Having greater self-esteem

Certification helps your customers hire people who are able to work with the products you sell them. Barbara Sokal, a training manager at Aetna, finds that people who are certified are able to implement better, quicker, and broader technology solutions than people without certification.[3] Certification saves the company money and enhances the career development process for employees. Additionally, data from Microsoft shows that 74 percent of people agree that certification is an incentive to complete training programs.[4]

If certification is so good, then why is it so rare? One reason is cost. Microsoft estimates it spends between $45,000 and $50,000 to develop one certification examination. The development process for a certification exam requires the skills of a Ph.D. psychometrician, as well as the time and resources to conduct extensive testing of the exam to ensure reliability and validity. Another reason is the legal responsibility you assume with certification or any other test. Certification implies that a person is skilled to perform a certain task. If that person fails, then you need to be sure failure cannot be attributed to the training. For example, if a certified EMT accidentally injures a person by incorrectly using a defibrillator, or a certified network administrator crashes a company's systems for five days, the injured party will seek recourse by suing everyone in sight. If the people responsible for the accidents were certified, then you can be sure that lawyers will challenge your methods of certification as a means to establish liability.

Evaluating Behavior

If evaluation of learning assesses whether learners can talk the talk, then the behavior level assesses whether they can walk the walk. Evaluating behavior, otherwise known as on-the-job performance, reconciles the key objectives you established for your educational program. It shows that the learner was able to transfer what was learned to actual performance. For example, if your key objective is for customers to use a food processor safely, then the behavior evaluation must assess how safely customers are using the food processor. To do this, you need to observe the customer using the food processor and judge how well he or she exhibits the behaviors associated with safe operation.

The key factor that differentiates learning evaluation from behavior evaluation is that behavior evaluation should take place in a setting that is as close to real life as possible, not in an overly controlled setting. The reason for this is that customers must be able to adapt what they learned in a controlled setting, such as a classroom, to the complexity that exists in real life. They must be able to perform the task while the noise of real life is all around them.

Data collection for behavior evaluation is typically performed through a questionnaire or survey. People familiar with the learner's performance, such as supervisors, peers, and even the learner, complete the surveys. Behavior evaluation should ideally be conducted on a before-and-after basis. Before the learner engages in a learning program, you collect measures of current performance. Three or more months after the educational program, you collect the measures again. To assess whether the educational program made a difference, you compare the before and after measures.

Behavior evaluation is probably the most difficult form of evaluation for customer education, because it requires extensive access to customers. This access is often impossible to acquire. Thus, customer educators typically punt on this level of evaluation and rely on the next level, results, for a more meaningful and valuable measure of worth.

Evaluating Results

For customer educators, the true measure of worth for any customer education program is its results. You want to know whether the educational program increased sales, reduced costs, reduced injuries, made it easier for customer service specialists and customers to communicate over the phone, eliminated errors, and a host of other key results. Results evaluation does not measure the customer's behaviors directly. Rather, it measures the results customers provide based on their change in behavior. For example, perhaps a goal for an educational program is to reduce customer injuries. To achieve this goal, customers needed to learn how to use their food processor safely. The results of a successful program would show that the number of customers injured in the current year is less than the number of customers injured in the previous year. See the studies in Chapter 7 for more examples of results.

If you did not do a good job of identifying goals and benchmarks during the analysis phase of the instructional design process, it will be evident as you try to measure results. Results measures require that you have known benchmarks against which you can compare future results. Without the benchmarks, you cannot show gains. And without gains, you will find it more and more difficult to secure the resources you need to do your job. The methods you use to evaluate results should be the same methods you used to analyze customer performance programs. If too many customers were calling customer support to resolve a certain problem, then you should once again examine the number of calls relating to that problem after you have implemented your solution. Similarly, if your competition was stealing market share, then you should once again examine current market share data to see if the slip has stopped.

Evaluating results is often difficult, because numerous variables limit your ability to draw strong correlations. For example, if you develop an educational program that improves customer product knowledge, how do you know it was your program and not a sales incentive program or price discounts that increased sales? In a big, fast-moving organization, you cannot control the introduction of these other variables. You cannot expect your marketing department to hold off on price discounts so you can evaluate the effects of your educational program. Businesses are not universities, where you can be true to valid experimental methodologies. Thus, rather than correlating your educational program to the overall outcome, address to what degree the education program was responsible for improving results.

In addition to results that are linked to needs and goals, also be on the lookout for side effects caused by your educational program. These are outcomes that you never planned for or expected, but that have either a positive or a negative impact on your business. For example, your education program might have helped a customer improve the output of their production line. A side effect might be that you increased the customer's switching costs to acquire a competing product, further solidifying your relationship with the customer. On the negative side, your educational programs might give a customer's employees enough skills that they leave the company to pursue better opportunities elsewhere. Be aware of the side effects your educational programs might cause, and be ready to gather data on them once they manifest themselves.

The results you capture by evaluating your educational programs will enable you to assess the return on investment your programs offer. Return on investment divides the dollar amount of increased revenues or reduced costs by the cost of your educational program. A result greater than one indicates that your program added value to the company. Be aware, however, that other variables will cloud your ability to firmly correlate your educational program with a specific return on investment. Return on investment should be your aim with every educational program you develop, yet knowing its actual value is extremely elusive.

Summary

The key points to take away from this chapter include the following:

- Evaluation is the means to assess the worth of your educational programs.
- Formative evaluation occurs after implementation of the program. Summative evaluation occurs after the implementation of the program.
- The outcomes of educational programs are effectiveness, efficiency, and appeal. These outcomes are evaluated on four levels: reactions, learning, behavior, and results.
- Reaction evaluation is how well customers like the educational program. It is also known as the "smiles test."
- Learning evaluation tests the learners' skills, knowledge, and attitudes. A formal method of this type of evaluation is certification.
- Behavior evaluation assesses how learners apply what they learned on the job.
- Results evaluation measures specific outcomes of the educational program, such as increased revenues and decreased costs.

References

Preface

1. Training (October 1994), 48.

Chapter 1

1. Stan Davis and Jim Botkin, *Monster under the Bed: How Business Is Mastering the Opportunity of Knowledge for Profit* (New York: Simon & Schuster, 1994), 42.

2. Stan Davis and Jim Botkin, "The Coming of Knowledge-Based Business," *Harvard Business Review* 72 (September–October 1994: 165–170.

3. Regis McKenna, *Relationship Marketing: Successful Strategies for the Age of the Customer* (Reading, Mass.: Addison-Wesley, 1991), 30.

Chapter 2

1. Claudia Gaillard Meer, *Customer Education* (Chicago: Nelson-Hall, 1984), 97–103.

2. J. Romiszowski, *Designing Instructional Systems: Decision Making in Course Planning and Curriculum Design* (London: Kogan Page, 1984), 80.

3. Robert Mills Gagné, *The Conditions of Learning and Theory of Instruction,* 4th ed. (New York: Holt, Rinehart and Winston, 1985), 219–242.

4. Needham, Harper & Steers Life Style Study (1985).

5. David Ogilvy, *Ogilvy on Advertising* (New York: Crown, 1983), 7.

6. Regis McKenna, *Relationship Marketing: Successful Strategies for the Age of the Customer* (Reading, Mass.: Addison-Wesley, 1991), 51.

7. John Church, "The Insurance Agent as Teacher: An Educated Client Is a Satisfied Client," *American Agent and Broker* 61 (1989): 38, 40.

8. Paul N. Bloom, "How Will Consumer Education Affect Consumer Behavior?" *Advances in Consumer Research* 3 (1975): 208.

9. Karen Matthes, "Customer Education: HR's New Approach to Better Service," *HR Focus* 70 (1993): 1.

10. Ibid.

Chapter 3

1. George L. Morrisey, *Management By Objectives and Results* (Menlo Park: Addison Wesley, 1977), 151.

2. Allison Rossett, *Training Needs Assessment* (Englewood Cliffs, N.J.: Educational Technology Publications, 1987), 29–46.

3. *Wall Street Journal,* July 28, 1995, B1.

4. Rossett, *Training,* 29–46.

5. John M. Keller, "Motivation and Instructional Design: A Theoretical Perspective," *Journal of Instructional Development* 2 (1979): 26-34.

6. Abraham H. Maslow, "A Theory of Human Motivation," *Psychological Review* 50 (1943): 370–396.

7. Donald A. Norman, *The Psychology of Everyday Things* (New York: Basic Books, 1988), 166.

8. Ibid.

9. Roger Kaufman and Sivasailam Thiagarajan, "Identifying and Specifying Requirements for Instruction," in *Instructional Technology: Foundations,* ed. Robert M. Gagné (Hillsdale, N.J.: L. Erlbaum Associates, 1987), 113–140.

10. John J. Keller, "AT&T's Secret Multimedia Trials Offer Clues to Capturing Interactive Audiences," *Wall Street Journal,* July 28, 1993, B1, B6.

Chapter 4

1. Kurt Lewin, *Field Theory in Social Science* (New York: Harper & Row, 1957).

2. S. Friedman, "Exec. Urges One-on-One Education for Consumers," *National Underwriter* 95 (December 1991): 3, 12.

3. Robert Filipczak, "Customer Education (Some Assembly Required)," *Training* 28 (December 1991): 31–35.

4. Judith Waldrap, "Educating the Customer," *American Demographics* 13 (September 1991): 44–47.

5. Rodney L. Cron, *Assuring Customer Satisfaction: A Guide for Business and Industry* (New York: Van Nostrand Reinhold, 1974), 24–25.

6. Mack Hanan, Peter Karp, *Customer Satisfaction: How to Maximize, Measure, and Market Your Company's "Ultimate Product"* (New York: American Management Association, 1989), 155.

7. Clay Carr, *Front-Line Customer Service: 15 Keys to Customer Satisfaction* (New York: Wiley, 1990).

8. Everett M. Rogers, *Diffusion of Innovations,* 3d ed, (New York: Free Press, 1983), 247.

9. Amy Lu, "The Complete PC Package," *CD-ROM World* (September 1994): 39–46.

10. Adapted from J. Schwarz, "Educating Away Privacy Fears," *American Demographics* 13 (September 1991): 47.

11. Sam Brown with Iain LeMay, Justin Sweet, and Alvin Weinstein, eds., *The Product Liability Handbook: Prevention, Risk, Consequence,*

and Forensics of Product Failure (New York: Van Nostrand Reinhold, 1991), 60–74.

12. Adapted from R. Bennet, "Campaign Opens Door to Safety Issue," *Public Relations Journal* 47 (February 1991): 28–29.

13. Ibid.

14. J. Weber and J. Carey, "Drug Ads: A Prescription for Controversy," *Business Week,* January 18, 1993, 58–60.

15. Carl Cox, "Customer Training Takes Off at Boeing," *Training & Development* 48 (December 1994): 39.

16. Claudia Gaillard Meer, *Customer Education* (Chicago: Nelson-Hall, 1984), 99–100.

17. Bob Davis, "Hundreds of Coleco's Adams Are Returned as Defective: Firm Blames User Manuals," *Wall Street Journal,* November 20, 1983, 4.

18. R.J. Reynolds advertisement, *Wall Street Journal,* October 19, 1995. A9.

Chapter 5

1. John M. Carroll, *The Nurnberg Funnel: Designing Minimalist Instruction for Practical Computer Skill* (Cambridge, Mass.: MIT Press, 1990), 10.

2. Richard W. Olshavsky, "Towards a More Comprehensive Theory of Choice." Conference paper: 465–470.

3. Edwin R. Steinberg, ed., *Plain Language: Principles and Practice* (Detroit: Wayne State University Press, 1991), 7.

4. Betsy A. Bowen, Thomas M. Duffy, and Edwin R. Steinberg, "Analyzing the Various Approaches of Plain Language Laws," in *Plain Language: Principles and Practice,* ed. Edwin R. Steinberg (Detroit: Wayne State University Press, 1991), 19.

5. Jennifer Thelen, "Mall Maze Illustrates Recycling," *Bloomington Herald-Times,* June 8, 1992, 1.

6. Jeanne C. Meister, "Retail U.," *Training* 29 (March 1992): 55–58.

7. Walter Dick and Lou Carey, *The Systematic Design of Instruction*, 3d ed. (Glenview, Ill.: Scott, Foresman, 1990).

8. Robert Heinich, Michael Molenda, and James D. Russell, *Instructional Media*, 3d ed. (New York: Macmillan, 1989), 38–41.

Chapter 6

1. Donald A. Norman, *The Psychology of Everyday Things* (New York: Basic Books, 1988).

2. George Miller, "The Magical Number Seven Plus or Minus Two: Some Limits on Our Capacity for Processing Information," *Psychological Review* 63 (1956): 81–97.

3. Bruce Nussbaum, "One Wrench Fits All," *Business Week,* June 8, 1992, 64–65.

4. Norman, *Psychology,* 188.

5. Ibid.

Chapter 7

1. Anna D. Wilde, "Nintendo? Bogus. But Investing? Bonus!" *New York Times,* October 29, 1995, 4-F.

2. Hewlett-Packard Co., *http://www.hp.com.* Portions ©1995 Hewlett-Packard. Used with permission.

Chapter 8

1. Al Ries and Jack Trout, *Positioning: The Battle for Your Mind* (New York: McGraw-Hill, 1981), 5–10.

2. R.J. Reynolds advertisement, *Wall Street Journal,* October 19, 1995, A9.

3. Microsoft advertisement, *Wall Street Journal,* March 15, 1995, B7.

Chapter 9

1. Michael Scriven, "Beyond Formative and Summative Evaluation," in McLaughlin, M.W., and Phillips, D.C., eds. *Evaluation and Education: at the Quarter Century* (Chicago: National Society for the Study of Education, 1991), 9.

2. Donald L. Kirkpatrick, *A Practical Guide for Supervisory Training and Development* (Menlo Park: Addison Wesley, 1971), 88–103.

3. Cyndy Fitzgerald and Celeste Boyer, "Driving Education through IT Industry Certification." Presentation given at the "Profiting from Successful Customer Education Strategies" conference. Chicago, IL, September 1995.

4. Ibid.

Index

TITLES OF INTEREST IN MARKETING, DIRECT MARKETING, AND SALES PROMOTION

For further information or a current catalog, write:
NTC Business Books
a division of NTC Publishing Group
4255 West Touhy Avenue
Lincolnwood, Illinois 60646–1975 U.S.A.